Guidelines For News Reporters

No. 516
$9.95

Guidelines For News Reporters

By Sol Robinson

TAB BOOKS

Blue Ridge Summit, Pa. 17214

FIRST EDITION

FIRST PRINTING—JANUARY 1971

Copyright © 1971 by TAB BOOKS

Printed in the United States
of America

Reproduction or publication of the content in any manner, without express permission of the publisher, is prohibited. No liability
is assumed with respect to the use of the information herein.

Library of Congress Card Number: 73-105973

Preface

In writing these "guidelines" I have drawn heavily upon my own experiences, observations, material presented at seminars and conferences, and the reports and suggested guidelines of such organizations as The Columbia University School of Journalism, the Ford Foundation, the news departments of the major national networks, radio stations such as WNEW, New York City, who specialize in news gathering and reporting, and the Connecticut Radio and Television News Directors' Association.

To the above organizations I am grateful for their vast contributions to the field of journalism and news reporting. Their efforts in behalf of the reader, listener, and viewer can be repaid only by the continued progress of a dedicated press determined to continue the quest for perfection in news gathering and reporting.

This effort and the earnest desire to keep the public fully and intelligently informed as to the events of the day in their community, state, nation, and the world will create the atmosphere that will result in the perpetuation of freedom.

Sol Robinson

Contents

Introduction

The mass media, like government and other areas of the establishment, has suffered increasingly from a credibility gap in the past few years. Some of this aura of disbelief is well earned. But some is not. It is for this reason that a book such as this can perform a valuable public service.

Misleading, inaccurate, or false information, like death and taxes, will probably always be with us, but intelligent self-interest is on the side of virtue in both the gathering and the dissemination of news. Accidental misinformation is more than a problem in communication; in today's complex world it can be a tragedy, or the cause of one.

It may seem the essence of presumption for a public relations practitioner to write the introduction for a book addressed to young newsmen and women, and on the other hand it may represent a high degree of realism. Most of you will spend a good deal of your time and energies dealing with press agents and PR people. Similarly, if PR or press agentry becomes your chosen field, you will be directing your attentions to the care and feeding of newsmen. Having been on both sides of the expense account, I have a healthy respect for the importance of the dialogue and the difficulties of maintaining it.

The relationship between the media and public relations can be mutually and socially beneficial. But the PR man who feeds a false press release to a newsman deserves the shafting he will most surely get. Similarly, media cannot expect that its needs will be met by the PR office which has found itself the victim of opportunistic reporting and chronic inaccuracies.

Beyond these minimum decencies there is a further necessity. Communication may be an art, a trade, a skill. It may even be a snare and a delusion, and it has most certainly become a cliche. But whatever it is, it is totally dependent on mutual understanding, not acquiesence or agreement or conspiracy, but understanding. There is, fortunately, a distinction.

The PR man must understand the needs of the media and he must translate those needs to his client. The media must learn as much as possible about the workings of the institution or individual whose activities are being reported. And both must go about their work responsibly. This does not mean that they must conceal or distort. But it does mean that they should each be aware of their own bias and hold firmly to a sense of proportion.

In the past several years, I have directed public relations for Danbury Hospital, a community general Hospital in Fairfield County, Connecticut. Perhaps hospital public relations makes one especially sensitive to the mutuality of the PR-media relationship. If so, it is all to the good. A hospital is an almost limitless source of news. It is also perilously dependent on the trust and goodwill of the public engendered, in the largest degree, by the media.

I have learned to value the relationships I have made with area media representatives (most especially the author of this book), and I have also learned a great deal from them. It is tempting to evolve theories to coincide with personal experience. Cheerfully, succumbing to this urge, I will offer one maxim for the potential communicator: To love one another may be asking too much, but at least respect one another. This is a basic requirement for anyone who wants to tell anybody anything.

This book will help you do your job and do it well, but more important, it will help you understand and respect your job. This is where credibility begins. A credibility gap is something more than a failure in communication. It is a failure in intent.

Mrs. Virginia Coigney

Chapter 1

The News Media

Recently, no newspaper, radio station, or television outlet has been immune from some of the most severe and serious criticism concerning methods of reporting current events. Politicians are constantly complaining that they are being misquoted; minority groups claim that only one side of a confrontation is being reported, and generally with bias; other groups are claiming that the mass news media is making heroes out of trouble-makers; jurists complain that the present method of pretrial reporting has a decidedly bad effect upon the lives and fortunes of accused people; there are some who claim that riots and disturbances are caused or certainly exacerbated by the methods of reporting and the unnecessary emphasis being placed upon minor incidents; administration officials are always accusing the news media of "leaking" stories that are without foundation or truth; etc.

Notwithstanding all this abuse and criticism, people are still buying newspapers, listening to their radios, and tuning in their television sets for the latest reports on the happenings and events of the day. What is more important is that today people are demanding that the mass news media report all these events as soon as possible, even while the event is taking place. They want, desire, and demand the "News" now, not later in the day or tomorrow.

With the demise of more and more daily newspapers (see Fig. 1-1) many of our cities and communities are becoming "one newspaper towns." And, where these newspapers used to publish several editions daily they now rarely publish more than one edition. Try to think back to the last time you saw a "newspaper extra." The Ford Foundation reports that the press system in the United States (Fig. 1-2) includes 1750 daily newspapers, 9500 weeklies, 9000 periodicals, 6000 radio stations and 686 television stations, with most of these operations deeply rooted socially and economically in their own local communities. Unlike many foreign countries who have some sort of national press and national broadcasting system, the United States does not have a single newspaper

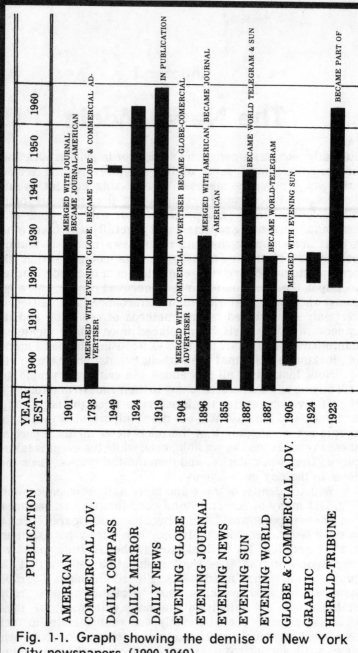

Fig. 1-1. Graph showing the demise of New York City newspapers (1900-1969).

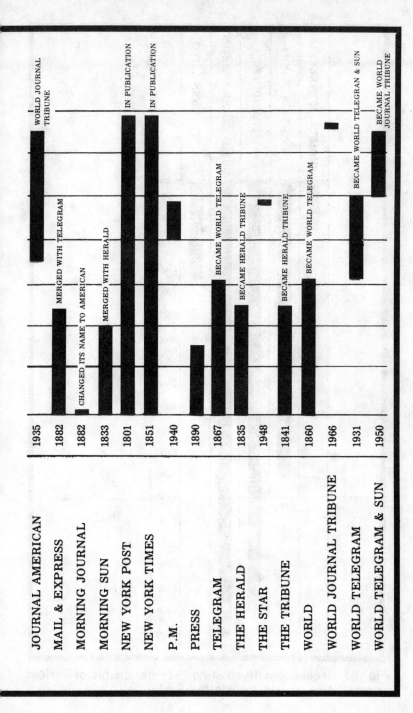

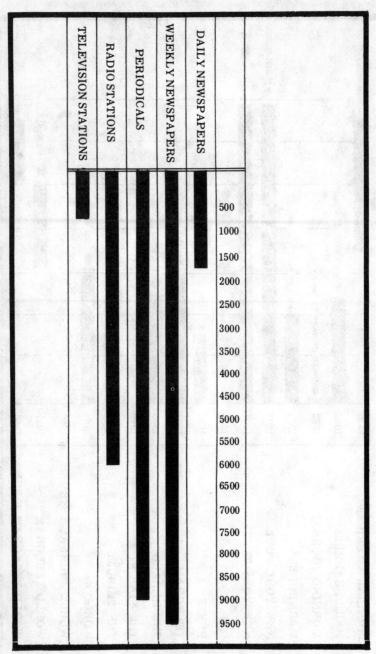

Fig. 1-2. Breakdown illustrating the relationship of various "press" services in the United States.

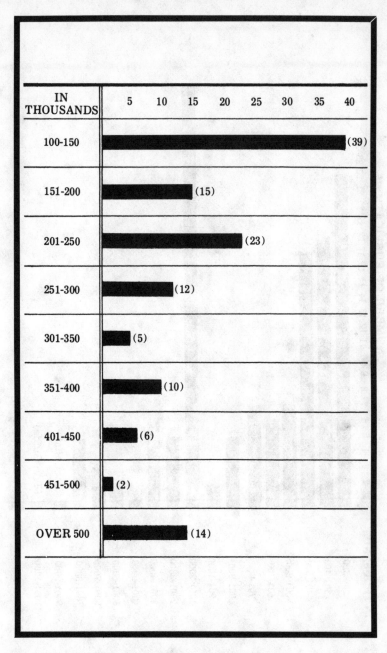

Fig. 1-3. Graph showing the number of U.S. newspapers with more than 100,000 daily circulation.

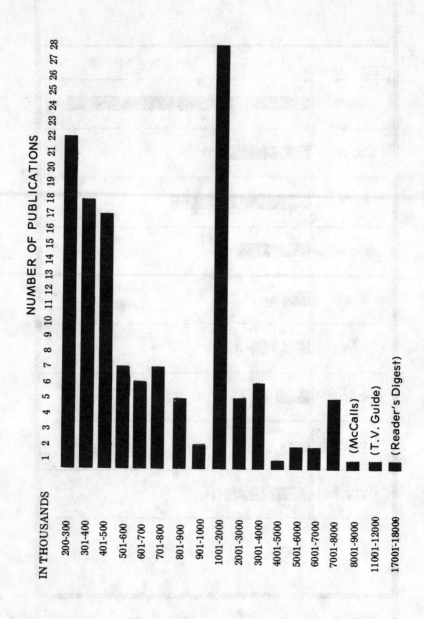

Fig. 1-4. Graphical relationship of U.S. magazines exceeding 200,000 circulation.

that has circulation throughout the nation and is available on the same morning it is printed. (See Figs. 1-3 and 1-4.) We do, however, have several radio and television networks which enable the mass news media to bring news events to the attention of the nation's listening and viewing public in a matter of minutes.

It is due to the demand for immediacy and the retrenchment of published news that today people are relying upon and are listening to their radios and television sets for the short "one the spot" report of news events and are reading their newspapers strictly for the in-depth coverage of the news.

If there is a single common denominator among broadcasters, radio and television owners alike, it is that the measure of success, both financially and in audience numbers, depends entirely upon the successful operation of their news departments. In fact, it is this department of the broadcasting business upon which all future successful operations are predicated.

When the National Broadcasting Company (NBC) was founded back in the early '20s only a handful of people, most of them part-time workers, were assigned to work as news gatherers or newscasters. These people were so poorly regarded that they were relegated to work in a 2 X 4 office hidden away behind the studio carpentry shop. Today, NBC employs a staff of over 1400 men and women whose sole responsibility is to gather, write, and broadcast the news. In 1968 alone, the cost of operating the networks' news departments rose to a record-breaking 150 million dollars.

With the proliferation and the increase in the number of radio stations (Fig. 1-5) practically every city in the country today has its "local" radio station catering to the needs and desires of its community. Most of these operations refer to themselves as "Your station for music, news and sports." They have become very popular, and audience surveys generally indicate that they have captured the local listening market. Most of the success in attaining this position is due to the station's programming and its emphasis on the reporting of local news. Researchers and industry leaders predict that as more and more UHF television stations begin to operate, catering to the smaller geographical areas, they may become the dominant viewing outlet of most local areas. (See Figs. 1-6 and 1-7.)

Because these stations operate in what is called the "small or medium size market," and because the greater

17

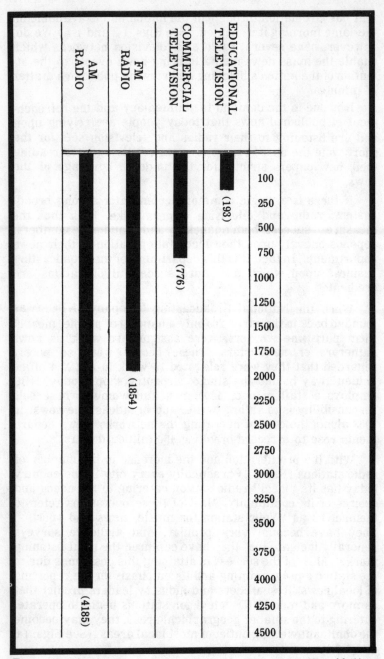

Fig. 1-5. Authorized broadcast facilities in the United States.

18

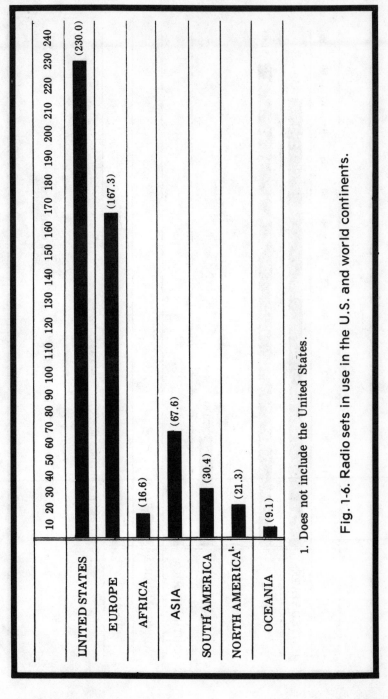

	10 20 30 40 50 60 70 80 90 100 110 120 130 140 150 160 170 180 190 200 210 220 230 240
UNITED STATES	(230.0)
EUROPE	(167.3)
AFRICA	(16.6)
ASIA	(67.6)
SOUTH AMERICA	(30.4)
NORTH AMERICA[1]	(21.3)
OCEANIA	(9.1)

1. Does not include the United States.

Fig. 1-6. Radio sets in use in the U.S. and world continents.

19

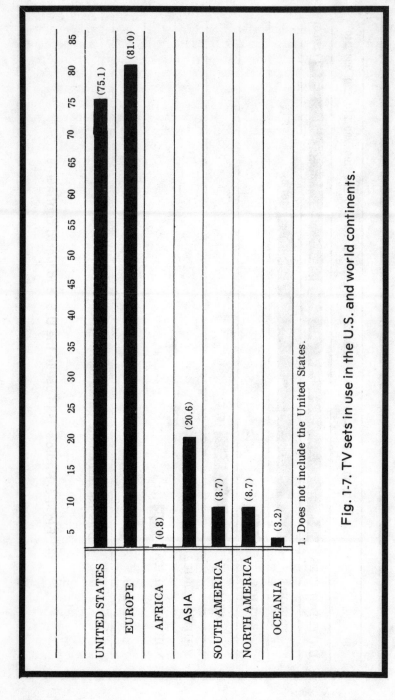

Fig. 1-7. TV sets in use in the U.S. and world continents.

	5	10	15	20	25	30	35	40	45	50	55	60	65	70	75	80	85

UNITED STATES (75.1)

EUROPE (81.0)

AFRICA (0.8)

ASIA (20.6)

SOUTH AMERICA (8.7)

NORTH AMERICA (8.7)

OCEANIA (3.2)

1. Does not include the United States.

portion of their revenue comes from a limited local retail market, they cannot afford, nor do they have, large news departments. They usually operate with only one person, generally called a "News Director" and rely upon "stringers" and their announcing staff to gather and broadcast the news. During the weekend it is the common practice of such stations to have only one person on duty, charged with the responsibility of carrying out all the functions of a normal operation: the combined functions of a disc jockey, engineer, and news department. Most, if not all, of these weekend employees have had very little or no experience in the field of journalism or news reporting. They rely heavily upon the newswire and on telephone contacts in order to prepare and broadcast scheduled news programs. Although I believe that everyone in the broadcasting industry who is involved in the pursuit of gathering or broadcasting the news will benefit from this book, my remarks are aimed primarily at those who are beginners or novices in this field.

Regardless of the news format used by a radio or television station, be it a 5-minute newscast every hour on the hour, or a 5-minute newscast every 30 minutes, or a 15-minute newscast three or four times a day, or any combination of these, the most important elements in fact, the only elements a listening audience desires and expects in a newscast are immediacy and accuracy. Now that news reporting has become such a necessity for the successful operation of a broadcasting facility many radio and television stations are constantly increasing the number and length of their news programs. Mute evidence to this fact is the recent practice of expanding newscasts in the prime evening hours to 60- and 90-minute programs.

However, none of this would have been done, none of these news programs would have been scheduled if broadcasters had not been convinced that there was a very large need and demand for such services. To meet this demand and need, radio and television stations have not only increased the numbers and qualifications of news personnel but also have had to increase the news-gathering facilities, or what is commonly called "the working tools" of their staff.

Radio and television news departments today use a myriad of implements that embraces the entire spectrum of mechanical and electronic devices such as tape recorders, telephones equipped with "beepers," two-way radio systems, "walkie talkies," mobile units, radio news cars (Figs. 1-8 and 1-9), permanent and temporary "remote" broadcast lines, police and fire communications monitoring equipment, air-

Fig. 1-8. Several WNBC New York mobile news units.

Fig. 1-9. WABC New York news unit covering a parade.

planes, helicopters, boats, etc. But, regardless of how much equipment or how large a news staff is employed, the cardinal principle behind news programming is that the listener or viewer desires and will accept only absolute accuracy (even at the price of a loss of immediacy) in the news report, which must be delivered in a precise and understandable manner by a newscaster whose voice is both distinct and clear.

As long ago as 1920, Walter Lippman wrote "It is altogether unthinkable that a society like ours should remain forever dependent on untrained accidental witnesses; the better course is to send out into reporting a generation of men who will, by sheer superiority, drive the incompetents out of business." I believe that with the schooling and training our present-day newsmen are receiving that we are producing such men and women who have added strength to the entire field of news gathering and reporting. A free and dynamic society like ours demands a well trained and experienced press corps who with candor and accuracy will keep it fully informed and aware of the news and problems of the community, nation, and world on a daily hour-to-hour, minute-to-minute basis.

Chapter 2

Accuracy in Reporting

Regarding news reporting one word is constantly stressed and reiterated: "accuracy." Irrespective of the quality or tone of the newscaster's voice, his technique or style, nothing, and I repeat nothing, can or will ever replace accuracy. You often hear people say "Don't believe everything you read in the newspaper." You seldom hear this said about radio or television newscasts. In fact, the most common phrase used in daily conversations between people of all ages, occupations, and professions is "I heard it on the radio."

Broadcasters will accept a certain amount of criticism or complaints about the lack of technique in presenting news programs, or the style or delivery of a newscaster, but they will never tolerate or accept excuses from news personnel for an inaccurate story. These men know that it is almost an impossibility to correct a story once it has been broadcast. Audiences constantly vary, and about 70 percent of the audience that heard an inaccurate report will never hear the correction. Immediacy must never replace accuracy; every news story must be fully checked prior to its broadcast. A good adage is "If there is any correction to be made in a news report, the time to make the correction is before, not after, the broadcast."

Under no circumstances should a newsman believe any unchecked story or one emanating from an unauthorized or unrecognized source. Failure to do so may soon cause your station to get the unenviable reputation of being a "rumor monger." This is especially important for those stations who offer money or prizes to listeners who telephone accidents, fires, and other news "tips."

Audiences take great delight and are quick to criticize whenever a newscaster mispronounces a name, word, or phrase. Therefore, a newscaster should never gamble on pronunciations. Any word, name, or phrase that is not familiar or not fully understood should be cleared and checked with a reliable source. Any newscaster who doesn't fully understand the story he is broadcasting should never expect to have his audience understand or believe the report. No matter how accurate or authentic a report may be, if the listener doesn't understand it, he is at best skeptical. Several such reports can earn the newscaster the reputation of being a "phony" or "hot air merchant."

The misuse of words or phrases can severely alter the accuracy of a report, also. There is a great difference between a "happening"; an "event"; a "disturbance"; an "incident"; and, a "riot." Take the sentence "State Police are now involved in ( ) taking place at the corner of Main and State Streets." Insert any one of the above words and you can readily see what happens to the sentence. All one has to do is refer to Roget's Thesaurus; he can readily see the multitude of similes there are for any one word and how the use of a simile can change the accuracy of a statement.

For instance, in describing a weather disturbance you can use any of the following words: storm, hurricane, tornado, wind gusts, wind blasts, gales, tempest, typhoon, etc. A good "rule of thumb" is never to use any of these words in connection with a weather story until you first checked with weather service officials for their nomenclature or definition of the weather occurence. To the listener each of the above words has a different meaning as to intensity.

OFFICIAL U.S. WEATHER SERVICE TERMINOLOGY
(Summer)

Severe Weather

Severe thunderstorm: Frequent lightning and damaging winds with gusts greater than 75 miles per hour (65 knots) or with hail three-quarters of an inch in diameter or larger.

Tornado: A violent vortex, characterized by a pendant funnel-shaped cloud extending from a thundercloud to the ground.

Tornado watch: An announcement that tornado development is possible in a specified area. All residents are urged to be alert to later advisories and take immediate precautions if a **tornado warning** is announced.

Tornado warning: An announcement that a tornado has been sighted or has been identified by radar. Take cover immediately in prescribed places that will afford the best shelter.

26

Tropical depression: The weak stage of a tropical storm with the highest wind speed less than 39 miles per hour (34 knots).

Tropical storm: Highest wind speeds of 39 through 73 miles per hour (34 to 63 knots). Not quite a hurricane, but nearly as dangerous.

Hurricane: A large revolving tropical storm (originating over tropical waters) with winds of 74 miles per hour (64 knots) or more, blowing counterclockwise around the center.

Hurricane center (eye): The relatively calm area near the center of the storm.

Hurricane watch: An announcement for specific areas that a hurricane poses a threat to coastal and inland communities. All residents should keep abreast of latest advisories and be ready for quick precautionary action in the event a hurricane warning is issued for their area.

Hurricane warning: An announcement identifying coastal areas where winds of 74 miles per hour or higher are expected or where dangerously high water or exceptionally high waves are predicted. All precautions should be taken immediately. Hurricane warnings seldom are issued more than 24 hours in advance.

Whole gale warning: Winds of 55 to 73 miles per hour (48 to 63 knots). A whole gale warning may precede or accompany a hurricane watch or may be used at the announcement for coastal sections adjacent to an area under a **hurricane warning.**

Gale warning: Winds of 39 to 54 miles per hour (34 to 47 knots), application is the same as for a **whole gale warning.**

Small craft warning: Winds and-or sea conditions considered hazardous to small craft operations. Winds may range as high as 38 miles per hour (33 knots). Small craft are identified as small boats, yachts, tugs, and barges with little freeboard.

Storm tide: An abnormal rise of the sea along a shore primarily as the result of the winds or a storm.

Clouds

Clear: Sky practically free of clouds.

Partly cloudy (or partly sunny): Three-tenths to seven-tenths of the sky covered by clouds.

Cloudy: Seven-tenths or more of the sky covered by clouds of sufficient thickness to obscure the sun, moon, or stars.

Overcast: No breaks in the clouds.

Partial clearing: A change from cloudy to six-tenths sky cover and implying an improvement of weather.

Clearing: Cloudiness decreasing markedly (by at least one-half) during the forecast period.

Temperature

Seasonable: Near the popular concept of normal.

Mild: Temperate, comfortable.

Warm: During the summer this term may even imply temperatures near or slightly below normal.

Hot, very warm: Extreme discomfort.

Slowly falling: Decreasing 5 to 10 degrees during a 12-hour period.

Rapidly falling: Decreasing more than 10 degrees.

Slowly rising: Increasing 5 to 10 degrees during a 12-hour period.

Colder: Temperature at least 5 degrees lower than that of the same forecast period of the previous day.

Warmer: Temperature at least 5 degrees warmer than that of the same forecast period of the previous day.

Precipitation

Rain: Of comparatively long duration (one half or more of the period covered by the forecast) or of unspecified character and duration.

Showers: Of short duration and varying intensity, with periods of no rain between showers.

Occasional: Occurring at irregular intervals.

Intermittent: Recurrent.

Scattered: Referring to area and not to time, usually implying that areas covered by showers total less than the area without precipitation.

Probability of precipitation: The chance (expressed in percent) of precipitation occurring during the forecast period.

Drought: This develops when the weather has been unusually dry for a long time, usually many weeks or months. Fairly brief periods, a few days or weeks, with almost no rain are usually called dry spells. The effects of the abnormally dry weather include agricultural drought, which occurs when the soil becomes too dry for crop growth, and hydrologic drought, which occurs when water levels are low in streams, lakes, and reservoirs.

Fog

Fog: Fine suspended droplets that obscure vision; may be modified by terms of "light" (visibility less than 1100 yards); "thick" (visibility less than 220 yards); "dense" (visibility less than 55 yards).

Smog: A fog made heavier and darker by the smoke of a city.

Wind

Very light: Zero to 3 MPH.

Light: 4 to 14 MPH.

Moderate (windy): 15 to 30 MPH.

Strong: 31 to 40 MPH.

High (gale): 41 to 74 MPH.

Hurricane force: Over 74 MPH.

Variable: Light velocities with irregular changes in direction.

Lighter winds: Velocities decreasing by at least 5 MPH.

Stronger winds: Velocities increasing by at least 5 MPH.

Gusty: Rapid and wide variations in the force of the wind during short time intervals.

Squall: A strong wind, usually accompanied by rain, that increases suddenly (to 18 miles an hour or more), maintains its peak speed for two or more minutes, then decreases rapidly.

OFFICIAL U.S. WEATHER SERVICE TERMINOLOGY (WINTER)

The word **snow** in a forecast, without a qualifying word such as **occasional** or **intermittent**, means that the fall of snow is expected to be of a steady nature and will probably continue for several hours without letup.

Heavy snow: A fall of 4 inches or more is expected in a 12-hour period, or a fall of 6 inches or more is expected in a 24-hour period. Some variations on these rules may be used in different parts of the country. Where 4-inch snowfalls are common, for example, the emphasis on heavy snow is generally associated with 6 or more inches of snow. In other parts of the country where heavy snow is infrequent or in metropolitan areas with heavy traffic, a snowfall of 2 or 3 inches will justify a heavy snow warning.

Snow flurries: Snow falling for short durations at intermittent periods; however, snowfall during the flurries may reduce visibilities to an eighth of a mile or less. Accumulations from snow flurries are generally small.

Snow squalls: Brief, intense falls of snow comparable to summer rain showers. They are accompanied by gusty surface winds.

Blowing and drifting snow: Generally occur together and result from strong winds and falling snow or loose snow on the ground. **Blowing snow** is defined as snow lifted from the surface by the wind and blown about to a degree that horizontal visibility is greatly restricted.

Drifting snow: Indicates that strong winds will blow falling snow or loose snow on the ground into significant drifts. In the northern plains, the combination of blowing and drifting snow, after a substantial snowfall has ended, is often referred to as a **ground blizzard.**

Blizzard: Winds with speeds of at least 35 MPH accompanied by considerable falling or blowing snow and temperatures of 20 degrees F or lower prevailing for an extended period of time.

The Weather Service uses the terms **ice storm, freezing rain,** and **freezing drizzle** to warn the public when a coating of ice is expected on the ground and on other exposed surfaces. The qualifying term **heavy** is used to indicate ice coating which, because of the extra weight of the ice, will cause significant damage to trees, overhead wires, and the like. Damage will be greater if the freezing rain or drizzle is accompanied by high winds.

Ice storms are sometimes incorrectly referred to as **sleet storms.** Sleet can be easily identified as frozen rain drops (ice pellets) which bounce when hitting the ground or other objects. Sleet does not stick to trees and wires; but sleet in sufficient depth does cause hazardous driving conditions.

Sleet: The term "sleet" is used to denote a fall of frozen rain drops which have passed through a freezing layer of air near the earth's surface. Upon impact, sleet will usually bounce and make a sharp sound.

Cold wave: Rapid fall in temperature within a 24-hour period which will require substantially increased protection to agricultural, industrial, commercial, and social activities. The temperature falls and minimum temperatures required to justify cold wave warnings vary with the changing of the season and with geographic location.

Blizzard: Generally, the term "blizzard" is used to indicate that the following conditions are expected to prevail for an extended period: (a) wind speed of 35 MPH, or more, (b) considerable falling and-or blowing snow, (c) temperatures of 20 degrees or lower, and (d) low visibilities. If any or all of the criteria are expected to be greatly exceeded, the term 'severe' is used.

Freeze: The term "freeze" describes conditions when the representative air temperature is forecast to be 32 degrees or below. A freeze may or may not be accompanied by the formation of frost and is usually restricted for use when wind or other conditions prevent frost. Adjectives such as "severe" or "hard" are used when appropriate.

Frost: The term "frost" is used when a deposit of ice crystals on objects is expected to occur. The process is similar to the formation of dew except that the temperature of the surface on which the frost forms is below freezing, though the representative air temperature may be above freezing. The frost may be classified as "heavy" or "light."

"Watch" is used to alert the public that a storm has formed and is approaching the area. People in the alerted area should keep listening to the latest Weather Service advisories on radio and television and begin to take precautionary measures.

"Warning" means that a storm is imminent and immediate action to protect life and property should begin.

LIBEL AND SLANDER

Both "libel" and "slander" are acts of defamation. Libel is expressed by print, writings, pictures, or signs. Slander is by oral expression. Any accusation that is defamatory, refers to a particular individual, and is made in public or is available to the public, or displayed for public view, is either an act of libel or slander.

One of the best definitions of libel was given by the State of Vermont Judiciary. The court described libel as an "accusation in writing or printing against the character of a person which affects his reputation, in that it tends to hold him up to ridicule, contempt, shame, disgrace, or obloguy, to degrade him in the estimation of the community, to induce an evil opinion of him in the minds of right thinking persons, to make him an object of reproach, to diminish his respectability or abridge his comforts, to change his position in society for the worse, to dishonor or discredit him in the estimation of the public, or his friends and acquaintances, or to deprive him of friendly intercourse in society, or cause him to be shunned or avoided, or where it is charged that one has violated his public duty, as a public officer."

Practically every State's judiciary has embodied the above definition in their many legal decisions concerning libel. According to these decisions the following constitutes an act of libel:

1. Any language which upon its face has a natural tendency to injure a person's reputation, either generally or with respect to his occupation.

2. Censorious or ridiculing writing, picture, or sign made with a mischievous intent.

3. Disparagement of goods.

4. False and malicious publication which charges an offense punishable by indictment.

5. False and malicious publication which charges an odious or disgraceful act.

6. False and malicious publication which tends to blacken the memory of one who is dead.

7. False, malicious, and unprivileged publication which tends to impair the social standing of a person.

8. Malicious defamation of a person by writing, sign, picture, representation, or effigy tending to provoke to wrath or to expose him to public contempt.

9. Printed or written statement which falsely charges or imputes dishonesty, or engagement in fraudulent enterprises of such a nature as to reflect upon the character and integrity of a person and to subject him to the loss of public confidence and respect.

10. Printed or written statement which falsely and maliciously charges a person with the commission of a crime.

11. Any writing that discredits a person in the minds of any considerable and respectable class in the community.

The legal profession classifies libel in three categories. They are:

1. Libels which impute to a person the commission of a crime.

2. Libels which have a tendency to injure a person in his office, profession, calling or trade.

3. Libels which hold a person up to scorn and ridicule and to feelings of contempt, impair him in the enjoyment of general society, and injure those imperfect rights of friendly intercourse and mutual benevolence which man has in respect to man.

The State of Tennessee's Court of Appeals has defined "slander" as "The speaking of base and defamatory words tending to prejudice another in his reputation, office, trade, business, or means of a livelihood."

Other definitions of "slander" rendered by the courts of several States and generally accepted by the legal profession are:

1. Oral defamation.

2. The speaking of false and malicious words concerning another, thereby resulting in an injury.

3. An essential element is that slanderous words must be spoken in the presence of another person other than the person slandered.

In connection with the above it is of interest to note that the State of Georgia's Court of Appeals held that "an oral defamation, heard only by one who does not understand the language in which it is spoken, is not "slander."

4. Words falsely spoken or another imputing the commission of a crime of moral turpitude.

5. Words falsely spoken to another imputing the existence of a loathsome and infectious disease.

6. Words falsely spoken of another imputing a person's unfitness to perform the duties of an office, employment, profession or trade.

Since the advent of the broadcasting media, and with practically every home at least one radio and television set, there is a trend in the courts today to treat both "libel" and "slander" as one and the same, not caring whether the statement is oral or written.

The following are some examples in which the courts have ruled that the statements are not considered "libel" or "slander."

1. Reporting a woman's age as 27 when she is really 35. The court held that to most women this is indeed a compliment.

2. A mistaken report concerning the death of a person. The court held that it is no disgrace for a person to die.

3. Calling a baseball umpire a "crook," "thief" or "blind bum." The court held that this is part of the spectator sport.

4. Accusing a man of being unchaste. The court held that unlike in the case of a woman, most men consider this a compliment.

5. Accusing a person of being a "careless driver." The court held that this is not being accused of a crime that is indictable. However, has it been written about a bus driver, truck driver or chauffer, or said about such a person in the presence of his employer, it would be an act of "libel" or "slander."

6. Statements made by critics, book reviewers, art experts, etc., if given as their honest opinion and totally related to the particular subject.

Following are some examples in which the courts have ruled that "libel" or "slander" existed.

1. Calling a bank employee or officer a crook or a thief. The courts ruled that this is quite different than calling a baseball umpire a "crook."

2. Accusing a woman of being unchaste. The courts ruled that, unlike the male, this is not a compliment but definitely an act of defamation.

3. Calling a person a "Communist." Most courts today rule this as an act of "slander" or "libel," although back in 1946 when the United States and the Soviet Union were allies, the Pennsylvania Courts ruled that this was not an act of "slander" or "libel."

4. Calling a stenographer or typist "illiterate" in the presence of her employer or other employees. The court ruled that even though the maker of the statement did not intend the remark as a reflection upon the person's competency it was made in the presence of those who could affect her social and business position.

Chapter 3

News Source Relations

Every reporter strives for a "scoop." Every reporter wants to be "first" with a story. But every veteran reporter knows that it is of prime importance to be "right." Volumes can be written about the "eager beavers" whose scoops turned out to be inaccurate and false. Inaccurate stories can be not only very embarrassing but can result in subjecting the station to a libel or slander suit. Here are some examples of the most common radio news reports and suggestions concerning them:

FIRES

Every station should develop the best rapport possible with the fire chief, chief dispatcher, or other person in authority at the local fire department. Such contacts can be very helpful not only in attaining immediacy in reporting fires but should be used in checking accuracy. Beware of the telephone "tip" about a "large fire" or, for that matter, any fire. If there is a fire any place that warrants a news bulletin or report you can "bet all the tea in China" that your fire department will be the first to know about it. If for any reason you haven't received a call from your local fire department contact, or if you don't have such a contact, be sure to call the fire department first before broadcasting anything.

I recall an incident involving a small radio station in a rural community. A farmer had received a permit and permission to burn down some old buildings and barns on his property. It was on a Sunday when the station had but one person on duty that the farmer, using the necessary and proper precautions, proceeded to burn his old buildings and barn. The station received a telephone call that a large fire was raging out of control in the north end of town. The announcer looked out of the studio window and saw that the sky was black with smoke, and through the haze he could see flames shooting skyward. Without bothering to check he immediately interrupted his program with a "bulletin" that the entire north end of the town was engulfed in flames. I need

An unimportant fire which destroyed old and unoccupied buildings: Constant news reports of this fire drew unwarranted large crowds, hampering both firemen and policemen; it also created a traffic snarl.

not tell you what followed. Fire afficionados from all over the county began racing to the area, people became panicky, the radio station's phones lit up like a Christmas tree, people who couldn't get through to the station were eagerly listening for more news about the holocaust but were getting only music because the announcer was too busy answering the phones. Police and fire department switchboards were overloaded, too. All of this should never have occurred. All the announcer had to do was call the fire department and by periodic reports about the "true fire" he could have created an atmosphere of calm instead of chaos.

Here again a newscaster should be very careful about his use of words. Adjectives such as "raging," "out of control," "very large," "uncontrolled," "blazing," etc., should never be used unless an authorized fire official labels the fire as such.

Another principle to follow: Once you have reported a fire in progress be sure to keep your audience fully informed concerning the situation. Don't let too much time elapse between the first broadcast and the next report. Once the fire is out, be sure that your audience is fully advised of it. It is a good practice to repeat such an announcement periodically within a 5-minute period after the first announcement that the fire has been extinguished.

Be most careful concerning your reports on the cause of the fire. Check with the fire authorities for their exact description of the cause. When in doubt use the phrase "a fire of undetermined origin." The use of the term "arson" or "suspected arson," unless coupled with a statement from a fire official, can create complications. Many times it serves no purpose whatsoever to report the cause of a fire. It serves no purpose to report that a fire was caused by "an explosion," or "faulty wiring," or "leaky gas stove" or "a defective oil burner" unless you can supply further details concerning the explosion or as to who installed the wiring and how long ago, or whether the "gas" was "bottled" or supplied by a utility pipeline, or the age and condition of the oil burner, etc.

The next Chapter discusses "style" and "technique." But a word of caution is necessary here. Be most careful of the style and technique you employ in reporting fires that are in progress. Fires are disasters and to many people the report of a disaster causes unnecessary apprehension. Be factual; be truthful; don't withhold important information unless so directed by public or other authorities; above all be sure that your "style" and "technique" does not cause a "panic."

A fire which totally destroyed the Frank H. Lee Hat Company Buildings: worthy of local, regional, and national coverage, since the company manufactures a nationally known product.

ACCIDENTS

As it is necessary to create the proper rapport between the radio station and the fire department, newsmen should also strive for such a relationship with police and hospital officials. Here again if an accident occurs that requires a "news bulletin" you can be sure that the police department or the hospital authorities know about it.

There will be occasions when you'll receive a telephone "tip" concerning an accident, and when you check with the police department they may say that they have no record or knowledge concerning it. There are many valid reasons for this; for example, the accident may have been so minor that all that happened was an exchange of license numbers or other information before both parties left the scene. The police were not called. Telephone "tips" concerning accidents should be handled very carefully. Question the caller to get all the information you can before calling the police or hospital authorities. Be sure to ask the "caller" for his name. If he refuses to tell you his name be doubly careful to check the complete report for accuracy. Ask him for the five basic "Ws," the what, where, when, who, and why. Try to ascertain the seriousness of the accident and make an independent decision as to whether or not it requires immediate action on the part of your news staff. The fact that a shopper sprained an ankle or even broke a foot, necessitating that an ambulance be sent to a department store, certainly doesn't require a "news bulletin" even if the store is located in the heart of Main Street.

Don't report accidents just for the sake of having something "local" to include in your newscast. A one-car accident (auto hitting a tree) or 2-car accident without serious injury or death to the occupants should be of little concern to others and should not merit news space. However, a one-car accident in which a utility pole is sheared off, causing an electric service outage affecting a number of people, is news even without serious injury or death.

When reporting an automobile accident in which a fatality or serious injury occurs, it is always good policy to withhold the names of those injured until you have ascertained that the "next of kin" have been advised. Too often announcers in their eagerness to be the first on the air with a news report about an accident have caused serious cases of shock to individuals who hear, for the first time, that a close member of their family has been killed or seriously hurt. Of course, I am not suggesting that you wait forever before releasing the in-

A two car head-on collision; no fatality; minor injuries. This accident is worthy of only a one-sentence local report. No regional report is necessary unless an injured person lives outside the core area, and then a one-sentence report is sufficient.

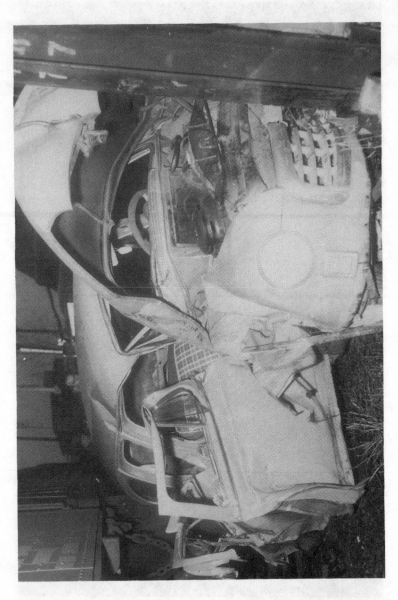

A one-car accident with a train, resulting in a fatality and train derailment: worthy of a local and a regional in-depth report. It is of local importance because of the fatality and train derailment; regional because of the railroad tie-up affecting commuters.

42

A one-car accident with a fatality: worthy of a local in-depth report. No regional report necessary unless the deceased lives outside the core area.

A one-car accident; no fatalities but it caused an electricity and telephone outage: worthy of local and regional report with emphasis on the outage and its cause, not on the accident.

44

A one-car accident; no fatalities; no injuries: not worthy of a news story unless it is to report on the driver's miraculous escape.

formation concerning the names of casualties. Create a policy concerning a definite time interval and live up to it.

In regard to reporting casualties, be careful that you don't start playing the "numbers game." Don't guess. Get some authority or official to give you his number or estimate and in your news story be sure to quote the authority. Usually the first report concerning casualty figures is seldom very accurate. In later and follow-up reports you can correct the figures. But be sure that you quote the authority for the figures that you report.

As in the case of reporting fires, be especially careful about conjecturing upon the cause of an accident. If you must give a cause for the accident be positive that you have a clear and direct quote from an authorative source. Also, be very careful about using a statement made by one party to an accident involving others. Above all else avoid the trivia; leave such minor matters for the indepth coverage media. On the other hand, remember that you should emphasize the source of the quote, the exact location of the accident, and the full names of those involved including their addresses whenever possible. Don't forget that there are over a million "Mr. Joneses and Mr. Smiths" in existence and there could be more than one "William Jones" or "Tom Smith." An address helps to positively identify the individual to whom reference has been made.

AIRPLANE ACCIDENTS

On December 5, 1965, two commercial air liners crashed head-on over the City of Danbury, Conn. Three people were killed and over 50 passengers were injured and hospitalized. The news director, a one-man staff at the local radio station, knew exactly what to do. Management had provided him with the excellent booklet "The Newsman and Air Accidents," available through the Aviation and Space Writers' Association, in Sarasota, Florida. The suggestions on how to cover air accidents helped him to get the news faster and with great accuracy. It helped him to understand why local and state police could verify only that an accident had occurred and refused to give him any further information. He knew that once a federal agency enters the picture, no one but that federal agency has the right to furnish any information whatsoever, and because of this knowledge he was able to contact and amiably work with the agency involved.

Too often the FAA, the CAB, and officials of the airline whose plane is involved in the accident seem to be uncooperative and "closed-mouth." The reason is that they themselves do not know what its all about. The chances are that the newsman learned of the accident even before they were aware of it. In cases like this the newsman must rely upon his own observation, investigations, and the observations of eye witnesses. A good newsman knows that eyewitness reports vary; that very often two people seeing the same accident will have two different versions as to what occurred. He knows that he cannot accept these eyewitness reports at full face value but can use them only as his basis for further investigations in the development of his story. Here again he must be most careful as to his statements regarding cause and casualties and should never conjecture, but should he cite causes and casualty figures he must name his authority as the information source.

HOSPITAL RELATIONSHIPS

When reporting on accidents, one of the major news sources is the hospital. Practically all hospitals today have a public relations and information director. This person is generally one with wide and varied experience dealing with the news media. It should be a simple matter to create an excellent rapport with this individual. A meeting with the public relations director should result in the establishment of a news policy for the hospital staff to follow if the public information or relations director is not available.

Too often newsmen expect the hospital's telephone operator to be able to give them the information they are seeking. Although many hospital telephone operators know more about what's going on in the hospital than do supervisors, etc., they should not be relied upon to supply factual information. Such information should come only from a hospital source who can be quoted and who is responsible and delegated by the hospital to release the information.

I know of an incident where the newsman of a local radio station called the hospital concerning an accident and was told that the victim died, that he was dead on arrival. As it happened there were two accidents and two different people involved. The person involved in the accident about which the inquiry was being made had not as yet been admitted to the hospital. You can imagine the problems that arose when the newsman broadcast the name of an individual as dead when he had only suffered minor injuries.

A good rule of thumb when deaths are reported is to repeat the person's name or have the informant spell the name. Be sure that you maintain a record of your call and the name of the informant. Even the newswire services can make mistakes; in one case the Associated Press dispatched a report that a state police officer who had been wounded in a gun battle had succumbed. The officer himself heard the radio report and was most furious. The radio station was able to conciliate him by making the corrections on the air and by sending him the teletype report it had received.

The reverse also can happen. You may receive a hospital report that there is no change in an accident victim's condition. Immediately after your newscast you may receive telephone calls that the person had died. Your only defense is to quote your source of information. But don't be too harsh on the hospital. They may be under a restriction of not releasing news about deaths until after the next of kin had been notified, so if your inquiry is made prior to such notification they cannot tell you. You can overcome this by having a working relationship whereby the hospital will tell you of the death knowing that you will not release it until the hospital tells you that the next of kin has been notified. If you can create such a rapport and understanding, never violate the trust.

Funeral directors and mortuaries are excellent news sources regarding deaths. Practically every mortuary or funeral parlor will welcome the opportunity to have notices of their services and obituaries read on the air. In small radio markets such reports are well received by the listeners as part of a newscast. Orthodox Jewish funeral services, which are held on the same day and seldom later than a day after death occurs, find that local radio newscasts are their main source to inform the Jewish population of a death and the time of a service.

CRIME REPORTS

This is one area of news reporting that requires the utmost accuracy. An error in reporting a crime can have a disastrous effect upon an individual for the rest of his lifetime. In reporting crime stories the newsman must be sure to quote his source at all times. Full identification must be made of all persons mentioned. It is amazing how many people have the same first, middle, and last names. If you do use names be sure to give an address or other identifying information immediately after the mention of the name. For instance, a statement that police have arrested Willian A. Smith and charged him with burglary places every William A. Smith in jeopardy. This can be corrected by saying police have

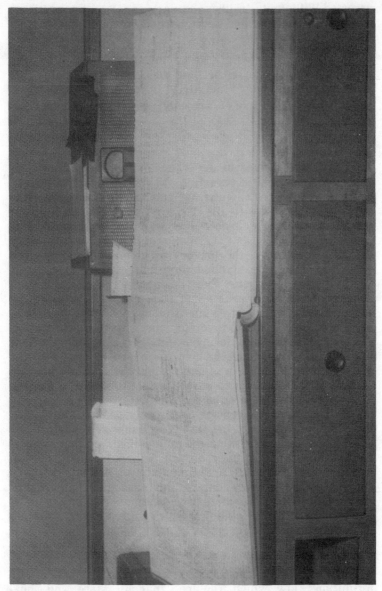

Typical police arrest book: Commonly referred to as The "police blotter." Entries indicate the date, time, name of prisoner, residence, occupation, sex, age, place of birth, color, marital status, height, weight, color of hair, color of eyes, arresting officier, charge, name of complaintant, cell assigned, baggage or property, and, disposition.

arrested William A. Smith, (address), (age), (other pertinent identifying information), and charged him with burglary.

You will notice that I began the illustration by saying "Police have arrested..." Never under any circumstances should the news reporter become the accuser by stating that William A. Smith of 34 Main Street burgularized the home of Dr. Fred Jones. The accurate report should be "police have arrested"; or "police have charged"; or "police state"; or "(name and identification) was arrested by or charged by the police"; etc.

This same degree of accuracy and source authority is absolutely essential in reporting "disturbance of the peace" complaints or arrests. Newsmen should beware of reporting trivia in connection with this crime category. Family fights or street brawls in which no one is seriously injured are just space fillers and can be very embarrassing to those named on the air. Remember, the privacy of individuals is involved whenever their names appear in a news report.

In the past few years there has been a rash of bank hold-ups, robberies, etc. News about such events is newsworthy only if a very, very large sum of money was taken or if the bank is located in the immediate or an adjacent community. Listeners or viewers could never be more disinterested to hear that a bank 10,000 miles away was robbed of $1000. On the other hand, if the sum was one million dollars they become attentive; or even if its an unsuccessful attempt at a bank in their immediate or an adjacent community listeners are interested. Getting full reports concerning bank holdups, etc., can be very frustrating. Because most banks are chartered by the federal government and are members of the Federal Deposit Insurance Agency or are National Banks, federal agencies such as the FBI are immediately called into the case. Once such an agency enters the case the local police authorities stay on the sidelines and cannot issue any news. It is a good practice for all newsmen to cultivate a relationship with those federal agencies who may be operating in their area.

At all times newsmen should maintain rapport with police authorities. Most states today have a "freedom of information" law which requires that all state and local governmental agencies make a full disclosure of their activities and operations and that their records are available for public scrutiny. In such cases the "police blotter" becomes available to all accredited newsmen. In making use of the "police blotter" care should be taken not to fall into the habit of using police terminology, phrases, or jargon. To you it may

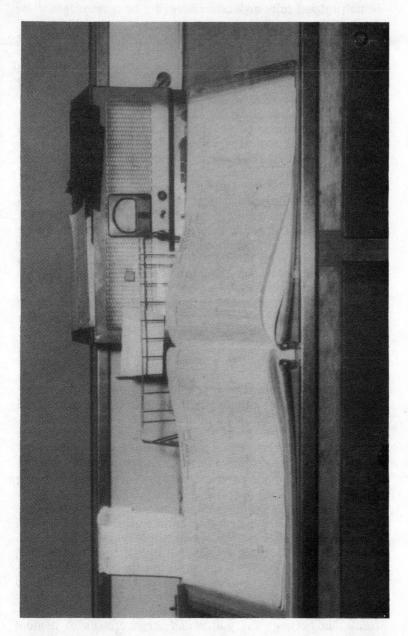

Police call book; sometimes referred to as the "blotter." Entries indicate the date, shift, time, complaint, and officer on duty.

be natural and fully understandable. To the listener it may be confusing, causing him to question the veracity of the report. Another thing to remember in making use of the "police blotter" is that not all of the identifying information is on the report. Carefully seek out the arresting officer, the officer on duty, or other authority for the full report and information and quote the source of your news story.

Many radio and television stations have police monitoring equipment. A word of caution is necessary here for those who use this working tool. Remember that it is a violation of the FCC Rules and Regulations to broadcast anything directly from a police radio broadcast. And don't make the mistake of relying fully on the radio direction to a police officer as your source of information. I cannot stress too strongly that you check with police authorities before any broadcasts. The police radio may direct an officer to proceed to a certain place where a fire, robbery, accident, or crime is taking place. This direction in fact is for the police officer to investigate and take proper action. No such thing may be happening. The instruction may have been given because of a telephone call or request which, though made in the best interest, had no trace of truth. The police officer arrives at the scene and reports back "false alarm." In some cases the caller is so excited that he gives the wrong location to the "desk officer"; therefore, the police car may be going to the wrong place while the incident is occurring elsewhere. Before checking with police authorities concerning their radio instructions you should also be sure to allow a suitable length of time before calling the officer in charge. Until the policeman arrives at the scene, makes his check or takes the necessary action, he cannot report back to his headquarters, and until he does report the officer in charge certainly cannot give you any information.

Generally speaking there has always been a most pleasant relationship between the press and the police; however, many people feel that the relationship is constantly being threatened because of the tensions created between news reporters and the police, caused by the media's coverage of riots and demonstrations. It is my opinion that such a threat to the usual fine relationship between the news media and the police is limited to only a few communities. What happened in Chicago during the 1968 National Convention of the Democratic Party can happen anywhere wherever there is a serious confrontation between the police and large crowds of demonstrators.

When reporting stories in the "crime" classification all newsmen should realize that they are operating under severe pressure from the police, courts, and the public. They should familiarize themselves with the famous "Reardon Report" concerning pretrial and court reporting. In January 1969 a set of rules, adopted by the U.S. District Judges for the Southern District of New York, went into effect. The rules specify that lawyers and other court personnel must not give any prejudicial information to reporters. Lawyers and court personnel are subject to "contempt of court" action under the rules. The rules, however, do not state nor provide for any penalties to any of the news media for printing or broadcasting any information obtained from lawyers or court personnel.

The rules also strictly limited the physical areas where news photographers or TV cameramen may operate. At the annual meeting of the Radio and Television News Directors Association held in California during December 1968 a very heated debate took place concerning the "Reardon Report." U.S. Judge Edward J. Devitt, Chairman of the American Bar Association's advisory committee on fair trial and free press pleaded for the news media to adopt the "Reardon Report." He claimed that the "report" was not an attack on the press and broadcasting but was a criticism aimed at the legal profession for being the main source of prejudicial pretrial information. He stated that "the main objective of the report is to stop lawyers and judges from talking too much about pending cases," and that "it is not the purpose of the American Bar Association to impede the reporting of crime news to the public."

W. Theodore Pierson, the legal counsel for the Radio and Television News Directors Association, in opposing Judge Devitt, stated that the "Reardon Report" aims for "Judicial management of the press far beyond the reasonable requirements of a fair trial for criminal defendants." He further stated that the report "attempts to establish the judge as a dictator of vital policy decisions of the executive branch." He severely criticized the report for providing dictatorial powers aimed solely against the press through the use of contempt of court citations.

In reporting crime stories for broadcast use, think the story over very carefully before putting it on the air. Be careful that you are fully circumspect and not a "headline grabber." Don't become the tool whereby trials are thrown out of court. Don't accuse anyone of "police brutality" no matter how badly a person may be hurt. The number of stitches to close a wound or "broken heads" is not an act of brutality unless the charge is made by the victim or his attorney. Here again be sure you quote the source whenever you report an alleged act of "police brutality." You as a newsman should never place yourself in the position of being the judge or the accuser.

RIOTS

This is one area of news reporting in which the news media is most vulnerable to criticism. Los Angeles Mayor Sam Yorty has repeatedly charged the mass media as being the cause of the Watts riots. He stated that television's coverage of the violent confrontations between the demonstrators in the South and the police exposed the people of Los Angeles to violence and the tensions the news reports created triggered the Watts riots. At the recent RTNDA convention Los Angeles Police Chief Thomas Reddin demanded that the radio and televison news people balance their newscasts between the sensational news coverage and what took place in totality. He said it was time that the broadcast news media stop making every incident look like a carnival and seem like a fun fest.

Looking for acceptable guidelines in reporting riots is one of the most arduous tasks. No matter how a newsman covers a riot story he is prone to criticism from many sources. Dr. Frank Stanton, President of CBS in addressing the Sigma Delta Chi at its annual convention in 1968 warned that the news services are in danger from constant erosion and qualification. He said that the journalists job is to tell the story of what is happening. And that means, all of it, the good and the bad, and the beautiful and the ugly, the noble and ignoble. Attempts to block this task, he said, will result in grave danger to freedom of the press.

Even the FCC is getting into the act with their rule that radio and television stations and networks answer complaints from listeners and viewers about their coverage of news events such as the national political conventions. A further threat was posed by Lt. General Hershey, former Selective Service Director, who threatened the news media by stating that inaccurate and stupid reporting of stories involving draft dodgers and other dissenters would lead to government control.

Every newsman has a tremendous responsibility to the public. He must inform his listeners or viewers fully and freely without any fear or retaliation from anyone but the listener or viewer himself. But he must be careful that in his presentation of the story he doesn't convey to the listener or viewer that he necessarily does or does not approve of the event he is reporting. Therefore, every newsman must pay the strictest attention to accuracy.

Here are some suggested guidelines to follow in regard to riot stories:

1. Remember that it is more important to be accurate than to be "first" with the story.

2. Always check every story received from a "stringer," friend of the station, or listener or viewer.

3. Never report the location of a riot or mass disturbance until the police have had a chance to "seal-off" the area.

4. Report only the necessary facts and details. Be sure to avoid the trivial or other events that serve no useful purpose.

5. Never broadcast any news which may create unnecessary alarm or panic.

6. Be sure to give periodic reports concerning the progress the police or other agencies are making.

7. Be sure to let the listener or viewer know (and often enough) that the incident is over or under control.

8. Never broadcast any report or statement without quoting a reliable source. Do not use the phrases "a reliable source," "a well-known public official," etc. If a person requests that you do not use his name in connection with a statement concerning a riot, don't use the statement.

9. Avoid the use of morbid or alarming details not essential for an accurate report.

10. You can get a more accurate and complete story as to what is occurring by posting yourself at a "command post" than by roaming willy-nilly all over the area.

11. Conspicuous use of television lights and radio equipment may add to the disturbance. If on-the-scene reports are to be broadcast during a disturbance avoid using film or tapes with sounds of screaming, gun shots, looters, or obvious inciters. These can be used in the follow-up stories, but their use at the time the disturbance is still active can cause panic or add to police problems by acting as magnets to draw large unwanted crowds of all sorts into the area.

Always remember that radio and television stations are in the field of communications. As communicators they have the opportunity and must accept the responsibility to build bridges of understanding between peoples. They must not only entertain but inform their audiences. Even more important they must be instrumental in assisting people to grasp the opportunity to create the proper relationships among themselves.

In this day and age, so beset with problems, news concerning struggles between groups, races, religions and nations is so eagerly listened to that it is the broadcaster's responsibility to report the news in such a manner as to diminish friction, alleviate fear, and create an atmosphere of calm and understanding. Only by careful preparation and presentation of "crisis news" can any radio or television station fulfill its proper role as a responsible member of the mass news media.

The National Advisory Commission on civil disorders stated: "The painful process of readjustment that is required of the American News Media must begin now ...they must insist on the highest standards of accuracy, not only in reporting single events with care and skepticism, but in placing each event into meaningful perspective."

Chapter 4

Style & Techniques

No degree of style nor the extent of technique in news reporting can ever replace accuracy. Radio and television stations can be criticized and even lose some listeners and viewers because of a lack of style or inept technique, but this is a minor consideration when one considers the trouble a radio or television can get into should their news reports be false or inaccurate. However, no matter how truthful or accurate a report may be, it will be the style and techniques employed in presenting the news that will in the long run determine the popularity of the newscaster and increase the audience of news programs on radio and television.

The first thing a radio or television newsman must realize is that broadcast news is far different from printed news. In radio it is written and presented for the ear. In television it is also written and presented for the ear along with visual reports that augment the newscast. Printed news is written exclusively for the eye. Practically all conversations between people are on an informal basis and all radio and television newscasts should also be presented on an informal level. We do not in the broadcast news field have the same access to techniques of the printed media. We cannot use abbreviations, punctuation marks such as colons, semicolons, or question marks. On the other hand, because of the relationship of the broadcast media to the listener, we have a better opportunity to interest him in our newscast and make him feel that he is actually experiencing or is a participant to the event being reported. We have the opportunity, unlike the printed media, not only to be factual in our presentation but to make that presentation, through the use of developed techniques and styles, in such a manner that the listener or viewer feels and lives the joy, the pathos, the excitement, the urgency being reported. But, the radio or television newscaster is at a decided disadvantage compared to the newspaper reporter.

People buy newspapers because they want to read them. Most likely it is the only newspaper in the house. If they don't like the way a story is written or presented they cannot look to another printed source at that particular moment. They have paid their good money for it and by gosh they are going to read it no matter what. On the other hand radio listeners and television viewers once they have purchased their receivers feel that the news programs they receive come to them at no cost at all and with no inconvenience whatsoever. They tune in only what pleases them and if disappointed or unhappy with the presentation can by the mere flick of a switch or the turning of a dial remove you from their presence and visit with another newscaster, and let us not too lightly gloss over the word "visit." For this is exactly what a broadcast news reporter is doing. He is there at the invitation of the listener and must constantly be aware of the fact that what he is saying is for the listener's benefit and not his. His choice of words and phrases must not necessarily be what he chooses or likes to hear. But it must be in the language that the listener likes and is accustomed to using.

LANGUAGE

All language or dialects, no matter how far apart they have grown over the years, belong to a language family. Of the approximately nine language families, Indo-European is the most important. It is divided into five major groups; Germanic, Slavic, Greek, Indo-Iranian, and Romance. Germanic consists of two languages: English and German. English is spoken in North America, the British Isles, and in the South Pacific. It is also the main language in regard to international conferences. Next in importance is the Romance group. It consists of the languages spoken in Southern Europe; namely, French, Spanish, and Italian. The Slavic group has three dialects; namely Russian, Polish and Czech. If Russia continues to strive for supremacy, that language may become a language of world-wide use. Greek, the language which most likely contributed more to the development of our civilization, also has three dialects; namely Ionic, Geolic, and Doric. Although rarely spoken today it once was the most used language on earth. Indo-Iranian is made up mainly of Persian, which contains many words from ancient Indian and Sanskrit. Surprisingly, there are many words from Sanskrit in Latin, English, German, and Greek.

Some other important language families are Bantu whose main dialects are: Arabic, Bemba, Bena, Chaga and Zulu. These dialects are spoken by over two-thirds of the black population of Africa. Polynesian is another language family whose dialects are Samoan, Maori, Tahitian and Hawaiian.

Oddly enough, there are few abstract terms included in their vocabulary.

An important language family which is not known to many people is the Semetic whose dialects are: Arabic, Hebrew, Aramaic and Phoenician. Yiddish is not included in this group, since it is a jargon of low German, Hebrew and English. The written characters of Semetic languages are made up mainly of cuneiform and the regular alphabet.

Altaic is also a main language group. It is spoken in the Far East, especially in Japan and Korea. Though read like Chinese it is related in many ways to the Polynesian. Its alphabet has 11 vowels and 14 consonants.

I mention all of the above so that the reader will have some idea where the English language stands in relation to other languages as we proceed with our topic, English, its origin and development.

OLD ENGLISH

Although grammarians differ in their estimates of the dates in which the English language developed, it is generally conceded that the years 450 AD-1150 AD are correct. In the middle of the 5th century, three Germanic Tribes, The Angles, The Saxons, and the Jutes invaded England and conquered the Celts who at that time were the sole inhabitants. Of the many contributions made by these invaders the most important was their language from which English gradually developed.

Strangely enough the Celtic people who were the sole inhabitants had almost no influence on the language whatsoever. In 59 AD when the Christian missionaries came to convert the island, they brought with them the Latin language which had a major and profound effect on the development of the English language and introduced such words as: priest, candle, mass, bishop, apostle, idol, prophet and sabbath.

At the end of the 8th and the beginning of the 9th centuries, the Northmen and Danes from the Scandinavian countries invaded England. The Danes eventually settled there and their language merged with and became a part of English. Some of the words resulting from this merger are: law, give, call, log, shirt, scrape, whisk, and scrub.

The Norman Conquest in 1066 AD had a great influence on the English language. William the Conqueror's victory at Hastings made the French great favorites of the Count and for over 200 years French remained the language of the upper class in England. The majority of the people, however, continued to speak English. The merging of the French and English languages produced such words as: hand, but, speak, teach, blood, yet, land and low.

Old English would seem strange to today's reader because the letters of the alphabet in use then are no longer in our present day alphabet. The Old English noun which was inflected in four cases also possessed an inclination in which the accent tended to fall on the first syllable of the noun, except those with prefixes. This tendency, called initial accent, became stronger toward the close of the Old English Period and is prevalent in the nouns of Modern English. The elaborate inflectional system of the Old English adjective is completely gone in Modern English. This elimination of the inflectional system is a large advantage that English holds over many other languages. The Old English verb had two simple tenses, present and past and was divided into two classes, the strong and the weak. In Modern English the strong class is the regular verb, i.e. sing, sang, sung; the weak class is the irregular verb, i.e. walk, walked. The Norman Conquest in 1066 AD resulted in the decline of the Old English Period and the beginning of the Middle English Period.

MIDDLE ENGLISH

This period in the development of the English Language lasted from 1150 AD to 1500 AD. Although the Norman Conquest was the main cause of the change from Old English to Middle English, its immediate result was to replace English as an authorative language first by Latin and then by the Norman-French of the conquerors.

This effect was threefold: (1) The social prestige of the Norman- French language and the extension of the church, with its use of Latin, brought into the English language an enormous number of words; (2) the loss of the West-Saxon written standard allowed free play to improve dialectal peculiarities and distributed the language balance of English; and (3) the influence of French and Latin did much to revise the traditional English spelling.

Research into the early period of Middle English can become rather confusing due to the fact that many important literary works were written in a number of dialects sufficiently diverse in themselves and made doubly so because of the individual spelling used by the authors. I believe that this confusion brought about the adoption of London English as the basis for a new standard language. Many factors played an important role in bringing about this change. Some of them are: the rise in importance of the middle and labor classes; the English Crown's loss of control over France; the gradual establishment of British naturalism; London government officials demanding use of the English language; the emergence of such widely read authors as Chaucer; the acceptance of the Southeast Midland dialect, used in London, as the written standard for the nation; Caxton's use of this in his printed books. Some of the words now appearing on the scene were color, honor, parson, image, attorney, five, suit, posion, stomach, ambush, archer, appetite, taste and veal. You can see the influence played by the Normans, the law, medicine and the military. By the end of the Middle English Period the verb was very close to its modern form.

MODERN ENGLISH

Modern English arrived on the scene simultaneously with Elizabethan and Shakespearian English. It began to make its appearance about 1500 AD and fully arrived about 1650 AD. When Wyclip translated the Bible into English he made the King James Version the most important literary work of the age. Only 6000 different words in the manuscript and it became a masterpiece of simplicity and one of the most widely read books of the times. Shakespeare must be given a great deal of credit, for his works had a great influence on the language. In fact he created many of the words that are still in use today.

It was during the reign of Queen Victoria with the many foreign alliances between England and other countries that the spelling, meaning, and even the conjugations of many words were changed in order to make them clearer to the Spanish, Dutch, French and Italians. But, it was only during the colonization of America that modern American English began to emerge.

AMERICAN ENGLISH

This language category encompasses all words and phrases used in America. Some of the new words which emerged during the period preceding the revolution were: political, congressional, presidential, etc. American English is fast becoming the major language of the world because it is charming, relatively clear, and has an abundant vocabulary. Some of those who should be given credit for this are Noah Webster and his dictionary, Charles B. Thornton who wrote an American glossary that is still being published today, Mark

Twain, Harriet Beecher Stowe, and Peter Mark Roget whose thesaurus is widely used.

SLANG

Slang is a kind of American English that is becoming more and more acceptable to the American people. There are three groups in this category. They are:

1. Argot: Usually used by the underworld, thieves, etc., to confuse the police or their victims. They coined such words as "stoolie," "casing a joint," "heist," etc.

2. Cant: Usually used by a small group or profession to confuse or mystify others. Many respectable trades and professions coin a jargon of their own such as the broadcaster's "on the nose"; "mike"; "jockey"; etc.

3. Slang: Although the boundaries between Argot, Cant and true slang are not clearly defined, a good definition is that slang is basically a vulgar form of speech not recognized in the literary language.

The history of slang is long; in fact some slang terms have lived for centuries and still have not been elevated to the acceptance of standard speech. A good example of this is "to cotton to" which dates back to 1605. Sources of most slang words and phrases are numerous and come mainly from gag writers; newspaper columnists; press agents; criminals; radio; television; newspapers; and the theatre. Most modern slang terms are short lived. Some slang words and terms have become classical and have been accepted into the language. The following list represents some of the newer words in current use:

Acid: L.S.D.

Angry young man: Author, composer or artist whose work is severely critical of present day society and traditions.

A-OK: Excellent, perfect.

Black power: Political and economic power sought by the black race.

Bug: A). to irritate or anger; B). a hidden electronic device used to eavesdrop on conversations.

Discotheque: An amusement area where people dance to the latest type of music (rock and roll, etc.) sometimes employing the services of "disc jockies."

Dolce vita: Living a fast life full of self indulgence.

Dove: A person in favor of ending a war, no matter how.

Ecumenical: The Roman Catholic Church's liberal attempt at Christian unity.

Escalation: An increase in any operation.

Exurbia: A community farther away from a city area than a suburb.

Fall: Artificial hairpiece worn by women.

Freak out: A withdrawal from normal or accepted behavior.

Freedom ride: Persons who travel to participate in civil rights demonstrations.

Frug: A new dance evolved from "the twist."

Go go girl: A featured dancer at a Discotheque.

Grass: Slang word for the drug marijuana.

Hang up: Psychological block.

Happening: Audience participation entertainment.

Hard news: A. serious news; B. national or international news.

Hardware: Military equipment such as guns, tanks, cannons, etc.

Hawk: Supporter of armed conflict.

High rise: Apartment or other building with more than the usual number of floors.

Hippie: Nonconformist.

Hot line: A direct telephone hookup.

Isometrics: Generally used in reference to exercises requiring the pushing or pulling of one part of the body against another object.

Kook: An eccentric person.

L.S.D.: Hallucinogenic or pschedelic drug; short for Lysergic Acid Diethlamide.

Megalopolis: Large urban area with overlapping towns and suburbs.

Napalm: Highly inflammable incendiary substance (jellied gasoline).

Op art: New art style that provides optical illusions.

Payola: A bribe or graft.

Pep pill: Stimulant such as amphetamine.

The Pill: Oral contraceptive.

Pop art: New art form using materials, printed objects.

Psychedelic: A). mental state associated with use of L.S.D. B). mass confusion of colors.

Retirement village: Community for senior citizens.

Splash down: Spacecraft landing in the ocean.

Swinger: Person whose tastes follow latest modes in dress, music, entertainment and morals.

Teach in: Demonstration, used by campus protestors, consisting of marathon sessions of lectures, speeches, etc.

Trip: Time spent under the influence of a drug.

Tuned-in: Awareness or favoring modern attitudes.

WRITING STYLE

This is an original trait with each individual; each person must create his own character or style of writing. But in writing news for broadcast purposes the newsman must remember that he is writing for the ear and for people whose command of the language may differ from his. He must remember that his story or report must sound conversational.

A good practice exercise is to take newspaper articles and rewrite them for broadcast purposes. Reading both the original and the rewritten article aloud should immediately show the difference in style. In fact all experienced broadcast news writers listen to their story as they are writing it. They then read it aloud to be sure that there are no difficult to pronounce words or that the sentences are not too long. A news writer must realize that many times he is writing for a newscaster or announcer who must make the copy interesting, entertaining, informal and informative.

Difficult to explain or important incidents sometimes require a lead-off sentence resembling a newspaper column headline. For example: "For the residents of Danbury, Connecticut, there is darkness tonight. A power failure caused by a fire in the main transformer of the power company plunged this city of 50,000 into total darkness"; or "City has a prescription for sick hospitals. The City today passed legislation that would place all hospitals under the jurisdiction of a public service authority"; or "The Supreme Court short-circuits the electric chair. The Court today reversed the convictions of two inmates of the state's death row"; or "Governor Dempsey took a look at where some of the state's dollars went this year. He opened the 200-mile Connecticut thruway." The first sentence, like the newspaper column headline, is the "attention grabber" that whets the appetite for the details that follow. Its purpose is to alert the listener to the topic before you burden him with the details. But be careful when you use a humorous, catchy, or fancy lead; make sure the rest of the story is written in the same vein. And, no matter how good your **lead** may be, remember **details** make the story.

At a recent seminar held by United Press International, ways to avoid several common pitfalls were suggested. Among the important statements made that day I recall the following:

1. Never start your first sentence with a question. It distracts the listener from the details that follow.

2. Don't make your sentences sound like commercials. You are reporting and narrating a news story, not selling tires, refrigerators, etc.

3. Never lead off with a quote. Unlike newspaper reporting where a reader can re-read a story to determine who made the statement, listeners have trouble associating a statement with its speaker if the two are separated. Obviously, they cannot refer back to the quote unless they have made a tape recording of the newscast. How many people do you know who do such a thing?

4. Never begin a lead sentence with a name. However, if you want to establish an important name early in the story, precede the name with the individual's title or some identifiable phrase. For instance don't begin by saying, "Abe Ribicoff, U.S. Senator from Connecticut, said today..." The correct way to say it is, "Connecticut's U.S. Senator, Abe Ribicoff, today said...". Longer titles should be broken up but the main idea retained. For instance, instead of House of Representatives Judiciary committee chairman, Emanuel Celler..." you could say, "Chairman Emanuel Celler of the House Judiciary Committee...". In the case of a high ranking government official the first name may be omitted if you precede the name with a title. For instance, President Nixon; Governor Dempsey; Mayor Lindsay; etc.

Because broadcasting today is an adjunct to living, most listeners are doing something else while listening to the news; items that require special attention should be very accurately identified. Avoid using pronouns, instead repeat the names of persons referred to in the story. Where quotes are being used, be sure to identify the individual before broadcasting the quote. Let us examine the following example. A correct story lead should read: NAACP Chairman (name) today charged Mayor (name) with sabotaging the low-cost housing project."

The same story lead incorrectly given could read: "Mayor (name) has sabotaged the low-cost housing project, NAACP Chairman (name) charges. Read both of these aloud to two people. In the first case, whether the listener was fully attentive or not he will know who is making the charge. In the second case, unless the listener is giving you his full attention he can very well, and most likely will, think that you are making the charge.

As important as it is to give as many details as possible, it is even more important to know what to leave out of a story so that it doesn't become too boring or unintelligent. However, never be afraid to repeat some background of a continuing story. In fact some repetition may be necessary because not all of your listeners are aware of or have a complete knowledge of every story. I was amazed at the number of people at a recent gathering in New York City who had very little or no knowledge of who constituted the "governing board" of a certain school district in the recent and much publicized school teachers' strike in New York City. The education problems of New York had made headlines for weeks and were the subject of several TV commentaries. If this can happen to a resident of the city, imagine how confused a visitor must be by a newscast that doesn't make some background reference. But you have to know how far to go, or repetition becomes a muddled quagmire of irrelevancy to a casual listener. What I want you to become aware of is the trivial and useless information that should be left out of a broadcast news story. Remember that you are writing for radio or television news programs. You must be able to condense in 100 words or less a story that takes the newspaper some 600 or 750 words to report.

Listeners are not interested in the ages of people in the news unless there is some special significance concerning the age. The only reason anyone was interested in the ages of U.S. Senator Strom Thurmond and his bride-to-be was because he was 72 and she was 24 at the time of their marriage. If both had been 72 or 24 nobody would have been interested. If two 28-year-old men were arrested for street fighting and one was critically hurt, the ages are not necessary in the radio report, but if one was 28 and the other 78, or if both were 80 years old, the ages would have some significance. If you do use ages in your story, remember you are writing for broadcasting and not for a newspaper. The phrase should be "80 year old Sam Jones"; not "Sam Jones, 24, etc..."

Among broadcasters there is some difference of opinion concerning the use of house numbers in radio and TV news

66

reporting. In a large city like New York, Los Angeles, Philadelphia, etc., it may suffice to say "Fire today caused severe damage to an office building on East 34th Street." There are many radio and TV men who think that even in a large city like New York the exact address should be given. They reason that with today's immediacy in reporting there are thousands of listeners who may have relatives and immediate family members working on East 34th Street. By giving the exact address there is an opportunity to allay fears and forestall panic. In smaller communities there is a majority of newscasters who believe that the house number is a must. Just saying that a fire destroyed an apartment in a house on Main Street is insufficient detail for the listener.

Speaking of numbers, remember that announcers must read what you write. It is permissable to use digits when referring to numbers under one thousand. When referring to larger figures always use words or a combination of words and digits. For example, "1,406" should appear in your copy as "14-hundred-6." When referring to money, round the figure. $10,827,643.38 should read in your copy as "just over 10-point-8 million dollars"; or "just under 11-million-dollars." As the news writer place yourself in the announcer's position and don't clutter up your typewritten report with a lot of numerals.

Never use abbreviations in broadcast news copy unless the announcer is to read the abbreviation as typed. Do not use BSA for the Boy Scouts of America. However, you can use YMCA for the Young Men's Christian Association, but never use Bklyn or N.Y.C. for Brooklyn or New York City. Of course, there are cases where abbreviations are standard. For example, St. Louis for Saint Louis. Also government agency initials like the FBI, FCC, FHA, FDIC, etc., can be used only if the general public is accustomed to hearing the agencies referred to by initials, otherwise use the full agency's name like the Federal Reserve Board or the Internal Revenue Service, or the Secret Service, etc. Likewise, the writer should be careful not to abbreviate the names of cities, states, nations, months, days of the week, titles of officials, etc. Just imagine if you were an announcer and were handed a bulletin typed as follows: "Pres. Nixon announced that this Sat. he will replace the head of the SS in light of his upcoming visit in Mar. to Eng. where he is to meet with the P.M. at his home at 10 Downing St. where they will discuss the problems of NATO with Gen. Schacht of Ger. and Amb. Russell of the Neth." The copy or bulletin should have read "President Nixon announced that this Saturday he will replace the Head of the Secret Service in light of his future visit in March to England where he is to meet with the Prime Minister at his home at Ten Downing Street where they will discuss the problems of NATO with General Schacht of Germany and Ambassador Russell of the Netherlands.''

Speaking of bulletins, don't ever fall into the habit of making a bulletin out of every unusual event. The firing of the head of the Secret Service is unusual but doesn't warrant bulletin status. Even when the AP or UPI wire services ring the bells of your teletype machine and label an item as a ''bulletin'' it does not necessarily follow that broadcast programs must be interrupted and the item immediately put on the air. The resignation of a high state official in California may be considered of bulletin attention for radio and television stations in California but it certainly does not warrant the same status in Connecticut. Connecticut broadcast outlets can use the story in the next scheduled newscast without their listeners feeling that they were slighted. And one important thing to always remember concerning bulletins is that the story must be followed up in greater detail at the first opportune moment.

The broadcasting of a bulletin that a plane has crashed must be followed up with full details as to airline, number of passengers, casualties, etc. Never broadcast a bulletin and then let your listeners or viewers remain on tender hooks or hanging in the air, wondering what it's all about.

The constant use of bulletins by many of the radio stations (TV stations rarely interrupt their shows) has caused some serious concern among broadcasters. Former White House news secretary James Haggerty, who is an American Broadcasting System Vice President, took the industry to task at a recent gathering of broadcasters. He said ''bulletinitis is the evil of the day and that the constant interruption of programs with sensational sounding electronic hodgepodge is causing the FCC to review news coverage and reporting by radio stations.'' The stress that the FCC is now placing upon this category of programming bears mute evidence to the degree of interest the government is taking. Broadcasters must review their news practices and policies and make the necessary improvements themselves, otherwise they can look forward to more governmental ''regulation'' of their facilities.

Good reporters know what to focus on and learn how to fully understand what they are seeing and how to separate the important from the trivial. Modern communication systems have speeded up the transmission of sound and pictures, resulting in an acceleration of the public's reactions to news. When a moment of crisis or a dramatic upheaval occurs it is far too late for a reporter to acquire the know-how to fully comprehend what he sees. The press has earned its title "The Fourth Estate" because it has influenced the emotions and broadened the knowledge of the people. Style is most important in "immediate reporting." A faulty style runs the danger of using our modern day methods of communication to distort and spread confusion.

TECHNIQUES

Some news gatherers and some newscasters are born with an inate quality that is often referred to as "style." World famous newscasters like H.V. Kaltenborn, Edward R. Murrow, Lowell Thomas, Walter Kronkite, Chet Huntley and David Brinkley, to mention a few, are examples of men who were and are possessed with a certain gift or quality which can be called "style" that makes them stand apart from the average. However, the technique in news gathering and reporting is something which must be acquired both by learning and practical application. In fact the Ford Foundation feels that even after a reporter has acquired the basic techniques he should pursue the quest for perfection by further academic studies either through fellowship grants or graduate school work.

The former president of Harvard University, James Bryant Conant, was one of the first advocates for graduate school work for reporters. He violently criticized what he called the "trade school" training for journalists. Dr. Conant and many of his adherents claimed that the journalist is a generalist best prepared by undergraduate schooling concentrating on the social sciences or humanities. Dr. Conant further claims that what a person gains in intellectual discipline and perspective will make him a better observer of the human scene, whereas anything he has failed to learn in journalistic work patterns can be easily learned on the job or off the campus doing the every day things that make up living.

Some colleges offer undergraduate courses in journalism which consist mainly of techniques such as typing, shorthand, taking dictation over the phone, writing and rewriting news stories, and the mechanics of editing. Other colleges require that, in addition to the above courses, the journalism student pursues a curricula that stresses the liberal arts. The accrediting body for journalism schools requires a concentration of studies in the humanities; the actual journalism function is a minor portion of the course of study.

The Ford Foundation cites Columbia University's Graduate School of Journalism, founded by Joseph Pulitzer in 1912, as the standard for the post graduate study of journalism. It is the only university or journalism school that grants a graduate degree exclusively in journalism. Its curricula steers a middle course between substance and techniques, with such subjects as history, economics, law, as well as practical experience in news gathering, writing, editing and broadcasting. Their graduate students cover public events, write stories or edit television film and prepare radio tapes. Yet, regardless of its excellent and prestigious reputation even this well established school has had to expand its horizons and teach their students the new techniques necessary to meet today's challenges. The curricula had to be altered and changed in order to adequately meet the rapidly rising standards of excellence, intense specialization and sophistication among reporters. The impact created by the television news medium requires that they teach students how to master not only the printed word but the elaborate mechanisms needed to record sight and sound.

The University has on its premises radio and television studios where students produce news and documentaries. These are analyzed and reviewed by the faculty. Students also produce a weekly half hour television program broadcast over UHF Channel 31 in New York City. Although there is a great demand from the broadcasting industry for many of the programs and documentaries produced by the students, Columbia strictly limits the broadcasting of such shows to the school's closed circuit television facility.

An indication of today's trend of journalist's preference's to broadcasting is the fact that in 1966-1967 of the 111 students enrolled, 40 chose to concentrate on the broadcasting medium. It is this type of demand that prompted the University to invite the former president of Columbia Broadcasting System News, Fred W. Friendly, to join its faculty where he now supervises student broadcasting experiments.

Another excellent institution is Northwestern University's Medill School of Journalism. With the help of a Ford Foundation grant of $1,092,000 the school conducts 3-month seminars for mid-career newspapermen; 3-day briefing sessions for editors, publishers, and broadcasting executives; tailor-made, specialized study programs of one, two, or three quarters for experienced newsmen who would spend varying periods of time on and off campus in formal or directed individual study, in research and writing, or in a combination of these.

70

Another program to be considered by the newsman who seeks excellence and aspires to perfection is the American Political Science Association's project which brings selected members of the press and young political scientists to Washington, D.C. for a year's work on the staff of members of Congress.

Not every publisher or newsman agrees with the idea of graduate school work, but they all agree that the need for analysis and for reflection has never been harder to achieve. Some feel that it is most difficult, if not impossible, to raise the performance quality of such a large number of people employed by such a great variety of employers working in so many various fields. Those opposed to formal study fear that improvement in the form of standardized performance will mean the loss of individuality and a narrowing of the display of new ideas. These men call attention to the fact that right now, today, there are strong forces pushing the news media and their employees towards conformity and sameness. They cite the fact that more and more newspapers are becoming a part of chains, and that the heavy reliance on standarized news services is making so many newspapers, radio and television outlets similar, thus driving the nation's press towards conventionality and predictability.

The editor of the Washington Post, J. Russell Wiggins, who is an arch enemy of conformity in news gathering and news reporting, has stated that individuality is not an idiosyncracy nor a quality that endears any news gatherer or newscaster to his more conforming colleagues. He expressed the fear that newspaper publishers and broadcast facility owners and staff members are going forward with such an adverse attitude towards individuality that there is little promise for its preservation.

Archibald MacLeish, director of the Nieman Fellowships at Harvard University believes that the method of improving press performance without sacrificing individuality is to heighten the perception of individual journalists and their employers by inviting them into the world of scholarship.

I have stressed the importance of graduate work in the field of journalism because today, more than ever before, the broadcast industry is seeking the most qualified and experienced news personnel. If a news gatherer or newscaster has any ambition whatsoever for job promotion he should make every effort to get as much education and training as possible in order to compete with the men and women who are now entering the field. An indication of what this combination of intellectual and professional training has produced is

71

evident in the findings of a recent questionnaire sent to the graduates of the Columbia University's School of Journalism. Of the 2000 living graduates who answered the questionnaire 1000 of them are today working journalists, 79 of them are with the New York Times; 36 at Time Inc; 23 on the Washington Post; 19 on the Wall Street Journal; 43 with the Associated Press; 34 with the National Broadcasting Company, 19 at the Columbia Broadcasting System; 18 with the American Broadcasting Company. Ten are Pulitzer Prize Winners and three of the last five presidents of the American Society of Newspaper Editors have come from these ranks. There are 152 alumni on college and university faculties, 16 of them serving as heads of journalism departments.

THE APSA PROGRAM

Schooling or post graduate work is not the sole means of attaining excellence in the profession, however. On-the-job, day-by-day experience also plays a tremendous role in such an achievement. It stands to reason that a combination of both is the most desirable. Today's journalist is challenged to look beyond the surface of public events, due to the fact that there has been a constant rise in the educational level of our readers, listeners and viewers. The over-crowded college and university campuses attest to this. In addition we have witnessed increasing complexities in the operation of our government. Unfortunately the deeper a newsman penetrates the inner councils of government for the real news and explanations the greater the dilemma he faces. On the one hand is the tremendous obligation he owes his readers or listeners to report his own independent version of the events; on the other hand he owes a debt of gratitude to and must protect the confidences of those governmental policy makers and leaders whose friendship he has made and who have briefed him concerning the events.

The American Political Science Association, which began in 1953 with the aid of the Stern Family Fund and has continued with the aid of the Ford Foundation, has the answer as to how to gain an intimate knowledge of government policy making while still maintaining loyalty to readers or listeners. Through their internship program eight reporters a year are transformed from an outside observer status to participants in actual confidential decision-making. Because he no longer is a "working reporter" he can with full sincerity make committments of secrecy to public officials without in any way compromising his professional ethics. He does this for one full year and, though this "on the job" training program is not the "end-all," it certainly should broaden his knowledge and give him a better understanding of the complexities of our government and the process of policy formation.

The director of the APSA internship program sums it us as follows: "Without some knowledge of such private transactions ahead of time, the public is often confronted with hardened official acts difficult to reverse; a consistent pattern of secret decisions makes democracy meaningless. If the reporter never is admitted behind closed doors, he may never be sure as to what has happened. He becomes dependent on the biased reports of individual official participants in the private proceedings. Such "leaks" are the calculated release of newsworthy information by an official who remains anonymous; the official selects what part of the total information to disclose, choosing the time and journalistic recipient for his own advantage and swearing the reporter to secrecy as to his source. The reporter may be tempted to treat leaks, and sometimes straightforward announcements, uncritically in order to increase his chances of receiving future important exclusive news."

An APSA intern spends six months of the staff of a representative and six months on the staff of a U.S. senator. Any worry or misgivings congressmen may have had about this program and about opening their innermost councils to newsmen vanished long ago. In fact there are now more requests by congressmen for these interns than the program can afford to fill.

Donald C. Baker, the co-author of the Sam Rayburn biography, who was appointed as an intern in 1961, sums up his experience as follows: "I came to be involved in things I never could as a newsman: in strategy, tactics, bargaining, pressures to change votes. As a newsman I had been on the outside guessing what was going on inside. But as a fellow, I've been behind closed doors when Larry O'Brien (Lawrence F. O'Brien, then special assistant to President Kennedy for Congressional Relations) was perched on a desk giving the facts of political life to some hesitant members of the House, facts like post office appointments they wanted, patronage jobs in the government, and favorite legislation they needed support for but wouldn't get if they didn't come across with their votes on some issues the Administration was committed to. I began to see that a lot of things that looked accidental from the outside were very carefully planned. But I also discovered that what from the outside sometimes looked like shrewd manipulation was sheer accident."

Baker, who is now syndicated in over 20 newspapers, often deals with his old congressional colleagues but he does so on a different level. He has learned that the old tried and true journalistic adage that "they who know the most are told the most" is absolute fact. He feels that today congressmen, senators, and high government officials tell him more than they do other reporters because they are aware of the fact that he has a full understanding about what really happens. He does, however, constantly have to remind his news sources that what he's after is material that he can publish.

SEMINARS

To become really proficient in the profession all newsmen, regardless of their educational background, should as part of a self-disciplined "on-the-job" training program attend as many seminars as possible.

The SREB Seminars are practically a must for all newsmen who operate in the Southern section of our country. It is part of a special Southern Journalism program operated by the Southern Regional Educational Board in conjunction with such leading southern universities as Duke, Emery, North Carolina, Texas, Vanderbilt, and Virginia. Because the South was the arena for most of the social changes in our country, such as the new black-white relationships, the fight against poverty, the mass emigration from the rural South to the urban areas of both the South and the North, the shift of labor from agriculture to blue collar occupations, the change of voting rights, and the clash between the advocates of federal control and states' rights, these seminars are designed to assist the newsman how to comprehend and meet the urgent requirement for perceptive journalism in a time of rapid and complex change. Factors that are peculiar to the South are thoroughly discussed so that events can be reported with more than a superficial knowledge of the region's history and contemporary life. This should result in better news coverage and lessen the resentment the previous coverage created. At the same time it would provide the expertise for a newsman of the South to become a credible voice of reality.

These seminars are open to news and editorial personnel of newspapers, wire services, news magazines, and radio and television stations. Those who attend pay the cost of their transportation. All other costs are paid by the SREB. Some of the topics included in past seminars are: The Emerging City

74

and the South; Latin America; Ethical issues in American Life; Administration of Justice; Crime and Corrections; and Urban Development Problems.

The Vanderbilt University Law Seminars are excellent for those who wish to learn more about the effects of the relevant Supreme Court Decisions and Civil Rights Legislation on the average southerner, especially those in the small town regions. Distinguished men like Archibald Cox of the Howard Law School, Dean John P. Wade of the Vanderbilt University Law School, and Fred P. Graham, Supreme Court reporter for the New York Times, generally head the list of lecturers, speakers and panelists.

Stamford University in California holds summer seminars, which last for a few days. Influential journalists from the United States and Canada are invited to appear. The summer of 1969 they held a 5-day session on comtemporary China which was attended by 35 journalists, including broadcasters; among the broadcasters were news directors, editorial chiefs, and foreign correspondents.

All these programs, fellowships, seminars, and conferences are important to the newsman. There are many, like Herbert Brocker, who think that "there is something about journalism today that can take a bright, ambitious, well-educated young man and within a decade turn him into a tired hack." I am one who believes, along with Ben H. Badikian, that we must create programs like those we have described that are directed mainly to individual practitioners, involving the whole institution of the printed and broadcast press who are producing a superior generation of newsmen, enriched, remotivated, and committed to the strengthening of the press in its struggle to satisfy the needs of a free and dynamic society.

TECHNIQUE

In the not too distant past movie theatres featured as part of their cinema program the then famous "Newsreel." Most large movie producers had their own news departments or subsidiary corporations with a staff and free lancers traveling throughout the world filming the events of the day. Some of the more popular were "Pathe News," Fox "Movietone News," and "Paramount News." Some featured slogans such as "The Eyes and Ears of the World." These "Newsreel" reports became so popular that "Newsreel Theatres" sprang up all over the nation. These theatres showed only news supplemented by a few selected "short subjects." Today there are but a handful of such theatres left, and those still in existence are usually located in railroad terminals or other travel centers.

75

These news pioneers soon realized that their paying customers, though intrigued and entertained by the news pictures on the screen, needed and demanded more than just the picture to keep them interested. They needed a good commentary to augment the portrayal. To meet this demand the film industry created the role of the "narrator" who, reading from a prepared script, related to the audience what was being shown. To find talent there was only one place that the movie newsreel producers could turn and that was to radio. For here were men with the necessary experience, schooled in reading scripts and whose voices were easily recognized and who, because of their radio exposure, were considered experts in the field of news commentary.

In a very short time the movie newsmen realized that no matter how expert the narrators, no matter how excellent their voices, audiences were more interested as to what they were being shown and not what they were being told. And a spirit of competition took hold of the industry. The movie producers also soon learned that audiences were becoming bored with listening to the voice of a single narrator for the entire length of the film report. They began to present different voices for different segments of the film and began to present the actual voices of the personalities being photographed. Of course, the newsreel industry began to fade with the advent of television and its emphasis upon news reporting.

This newest entry (TV) into the mass news media field began and progressed like its predecessors. Taking the best it could find from both the radio and newsreel field it began to develop a technique of its own. At the beginning the television news program featured a single commentator, or newsman, reading from a prepared script supplemented with a few "still" photographs. These news programs seldom were more than 15 minutes in duration, and many were even shorter. But, as the listening audience began to demand more complete coverage and because events of the day were moving so rapidly, the length of such news programs was extended to a half hour, then a full hour, and now even to an hour and a half. And, as the movie newsreel men and radio program directors learned, television producers soon realized that the listening public, no matter how enamoured they might have been with a certain personality, easily became bored and disinterested unless there were more than one or two or three different voices and personalities on the video screen speaking to them. Television news teams began to make their appearance and the main voice instead of being the narrator now became the "anchor man" who through the genius of our modern day electronics began to present newsmen, personalities and pictures from every section of the globe. The prime instrument that allows this miracle to be presented in such a commonly accepted manner is the tape recorder.

TAPE RECORDING

The miraculous advances made with this electronic marvel, from its reduction is physical size to the techniques of splicing and the use of cartridges, is a most fascinating story that in itself would require a volume to relate. Our concern here, however, is how a newsman can and should use this instrument.

Psychologists agree that the presentation of a 3-minute picture with sound has a greater and more lasting effect than a thousand word report in a newspaper. Picture for yourself the image a person conjures up for himself when he hears a Stokely Carmichael or Rapp Brown shouting "Burn Baby Burn," then try to get the same effect reading a newspaper report of either of these men making the same statement. All the newspaper reports or magazine articles about the 1968 Democratic National Convention in Chicago can be rolled up into one and have less of an effect than did the 15-minute, or shorter, on-the-spot television report. Could any newspaper report on the assassination of U.S. Senator Robert Kennedy have had the same effect, no matter how well written, as did the actual event as portrayed in picture and sound on the television screen or on the radio receiver?

There is no doubt that the proper use of the tape recorder and the presentation of tape reports enhances any news program. Its possibilities are limitless. But, the improper use of this vehicle can destroy the best planned news program. Radio and television newsmen must know both how and when to use tape reports and, even more important, how and when not to use tape. We will now endeavor to suggest some methods for the use of this vehicle and some of the errors made by the novices is using tape reports.

Tape reports should be used as a supplement to the story and not as the story itself. Each tape report should be preceded and followed by a closing statement from the newscaster. For instance, let us take a news report concerning a hold-up in which deaths occurred (If there were no deaths, or if the hold-up was not of major importance, there would be no excuse for this as a news story).

Newscaster: "The hoodlums who have been plaguing our city with a rash of hold-ups met their waterloo today when they attempted to rob the State Street Liquor Store. Here is the owner, John Smith, with his account of what happened."

Tape: (John Smith's report)

Newscaster: "The outcome of the shooting resulted in the death of two of the gunmen (names, etc., if available). Seriously wounded was patrolman Ed Brown (whose condition is now reported by the hospital authorities as serious, or other information if available). The police are now searching for the driver of the get-away car who escaped during the fracas."

The above method is the correct way to use tape in reporting such an instance. Here is the incorrect way:

Newscaster: The hoodlums who have been plaguing our city with a rash of hold-ups met their waterloo today when they attempted to rob the State Street Liquor Store. Police entered the premises soon after two gunmen ordered the store's proprietor, John Smith, to hand over the money in the cash register. The surprised hold-up men opened up on the police who returned their fire, killing both hoodlums. In the fracas patrolman Ed Brown was seriously wounded and is now reported to be resting comfortably. A third gunman, who apparently was the driver of the get-away car, escaped and is now being hunted by the police. Here on tape is John Smith, proprietor of the State Street Liquor Store, with his account of what happened."

Tape: (John Smith's report)

Newscaster: "That was John Smith, proprietor of the State Street Liquor Store telling us what happened when he was held up today."

You can readily see that the tape report by John Smith could not add anything to the story. At best it could only be a repetition of what was already said. This is also true of the novice newscaster who reports everything that a politician says in his statement and then presents a tape report in which the politician repeats the entire statement. A good newscaster knows how and when, and when not, to use tape reports in a newscast. It is this knowledge which makes the difference between a good and a bad news reporter.

The length of the tape report is also most important. The average person speaks at the rate of 100 to 125 words per minute. Twenty seconds of sound on the radio or television is a long time. Experiment and try to be silent for 20 to 30 seconds. It will seem like an eternity. Unless the tape report is the entire story, try to limit all tape reports to a maximum of 40 to 45 seconds. And, above all, remember that not all people speak intelligently and with clarity. Don't program tape reports in your newscast just for the sake of adding another voice. It must have content and clarity. The absence of either will destroy not only that particular story but may well destroy the entire newscast.

When speaking of the length of tape reports I am not suggesting that you limit the length of the report at the time you make the tape. I am speaking about the use of the recording. When making the recording get as much on the tape as it is possible. Then edit, and, I mean edit. There is no rule which says that a newsman must use everything he has recorded. He doesn't have to run the gamut from alpha to the omega. He can and should use excerpts interspersed with his own report.

Many radio newsmen in covering fires make the mistake of always having the chief make a tape for the newscast. The news report of the fire becomes clogged with all kinds of statistics as to the number of fire engines called out, the size and length of the fire hose used, who reported the fire and how soon the firemen arrived on the scene. Unless the chief can give you pertinent information as to the cause of the fire, an estimate of the damage, etc., and do it in a clear and understandable manner, a report prepared by yourself and delivered properly should be used. In using tape reports you should apply criteria suggested earlier: Does the use of "tape" enhance or add to the newscast? If for any reason it should detract from the story or the quality of the newscast, throw the tape away.

Today, everyone knows that all radio and television stations have tape recorders. It isn't necessary for you to indicate this to your audience by the constant use of the equipment. Develop the technique necessary to obtain the maximum results from its use, always bearing in mind that though it can enhance your newscast the misuse of this piece of electronic equipment can destroy not only your newscast but your image as a news reporter.

We have discussed the use of tape as part of a newscast. Let us now consider the use of a tape recorder by the newsman who is covering an event. There are preparations that must be made before going out on the assignment. Many of these are academic yet are so often overlooked that they bear repetition at this time.

All equipment must be checked before you leave for the assignment. Don't rely on others to do this for you. Do it yourself. Imagine how embarrassing it will be to arrive at the scene and find out that your tape recorder is inoperative. The fact that some engineer back at the station told you that it was OK will not solve your problem at that moment. If you are using a battery-operated recorder, check the batteries yourself. Test the recorder to make sure it's working and that you have a spare set of batteries. If you are to use electric current, check that you have enough extension cords to meet all emergencies that may arise. Check the microphone, especially the microphone plug for frayed ends which may cause a short circuit, and be sure that you take along a sufficient length of microphone cord.

Remember your "deadline." If you are covering an event for a 12 noon broadcast be sure that you return in sufficient time to allow for editing and the inclusion of your tape report in the newscast. Don't be afraid to make several recordings with different versions of the activity taking place. Although not every version will be used the news director will have a choice and can use the other versions on subsequent newscasts. But don't be too lengthy in your reports. Editing is time consuming to say the least, especially when there is a deadline to meet.

Avoid the extraneous, especially cute or flowery phrases. Get and report the facts. The newsman back at the studio will supply the clever lead-ins. But, be sure that you capture on tape those things which the writer can't supply. The tape recorder was created to capture sounds and voices. These sounds and voices will enhance the newscast.

Know exactly where you are going. If the event you are covering is taking place in a large hotel be sure you know exactly where and in what part of the hotel the room is located. And allow yourself sufficient time not only to get there and set up your equipment but also enough time to gather your equipment and report back to the studio or newsroom.

Know what you are supposed to cover. If it's an event try to get some background on it. If it's a personality that you haven't met before be sure to get a description of the individual. It's an old chestnut, but volumes could be filled about reporters ignoring the principal and greeting bystand-ers as Mr. Congressman, etc. Ask if there are any special or specific reports or questions that you are to obtain. But don't make the mistake of only asking those specific questions. If you are not satisfied with the clarity of the answer or report ask it again. Put yourself in the position of the listener to the newscast. If you are confused, he certainly will be. If you are not satisfied, he certainly won't be satisfied.

Be sure that within the time limitations you get the complete report or story. If it's a public event every newsman present will get the same facts at the same time. Don't make the error of trying for a "scoop" or "newsbeat" by leaving too soon. If time permits wait for the meeting to end and break up. Too often what is said after a formal meeting ends is more newsworthy than what was said during the meeting.

Observe the veteran newsmen and reporters. See who they seek out and what information they are trying to elicit. Don't make the mistake of accepting the enthusiasm of youth at the expense of ignoring the experience of the veterans.

Chapter 5

The News Media
&
The Minorities

Stories of violence and tragedy have become a traditional part of most news reports. This might be due to the fact that the emotional urges and cross purposes of personalities, and "causes" that result in violence or tragedy, lend themselves so well to news reporting. Of course, a newsman should never foresake the factual for the sake of sensationalism. In any news report one tragedy or act of violence, or at the most two, is more than sufficient for the average listener or viewer. Too many more such stories in one news report tend not only to clutter up the newscast but succeed in confusing the sequence of reports concerning minor or major news events.

Mikhail Bakunin, the famous Russian anarchist in his "Dieu Etl'etat" states: "The liberty of man consists solely in this, that he obeys the laws of nature because he has himself recognized them as such and not because they have been imposed upon him externally by any foreign will whatever, be it divine, collective or individual." The prime law of nature is that man, though classifed as an animal, is in fact a human being. He is a human being whether his skin is white, black, red or yellow. This is most important for all newsmen to remember. The news treatment given minority groups should not be dictated by the edicts of man, collective or individual.

Because many of our cities across our nation have been wracked with rioting, looting and arson Americans began to face-up to such questions as: "Are whites morally obligated to help negroes advance?" "Should there be a massive program to open new job opportunities for negroes?" "What should individual industries do about the situation?"

The Federal Communications Commission and the entire broadcasting industry began, likewise, to question their attitudes and employment practices of not only the black minority group but other minority groups such as the spanish-speaking people. Late in 1968 the FCC issued a directive to all radio and television stations under their jurisdiction that they must make every effort to involve and employ members of these minority groups in every phase of their operations, and the one particular phase to be given top priority was the news department.

Leaders of minority groups were complaining that the white newsman and commentator did not understand their problems nor the goals they were seeking to achieve. They made the very blunt statement that only a black man knows what a black man feels and wants; that only a black man is trusted by black men and no white reporter can ever get the true or real story.

This may or may not be true; nevertheless, enough pressure has been brought to bear on management that today we have more black reporters and newscasters employed in the broadcasting industry than ever before. But what of the white reporter. Is he to be relegated to report and gather news of only the white community? Is he to be considered totally incompetent to report upon any happening or occurrence in the black community? I am among those who say that this is not necessarily so. A good reporter or newscaster, be he white or black, is still a good reporter or newscaster. A poor one will still be a poor one regardless of the color of his skin. For if we are to accept the premise that only blacks can report about blacks then we must begin to think in terms of only women reporting about women and men reporting about men.

This does not, however, mean that all white reporters have complete expertise and ability to report on the concerns and activities of minority groups. So, the purpose of this chapter is to assist those to attain this expertise and ability and to suggest workable guidelines toward achieving this goal.

BACKGROUND

Of prime importance is that every newsman have a thorough knowledge of the background and events that have brought us to the present situation concerning civil rights. He must know that black people have been in the United States since the early days of its colonization and that, with envy and dismay, they have seen generations of white refugees from Europe's serfdom and discrimination arrive here and make good while they were kept in a state of bondage and relegated to the slums and the ghettos. For over two centuries most blacks in the United States were bought and sold as mere merchandise or chattels. And then, when a few of them began to achieve some status and position after the Emancipation Proclamation, there was a white backlash which practically stripped them of every right they had gained. It was only in the late 1950s and the 1960s that legislation was passed to try and restore most of those rights. Then began the second wave of the white backlash that has stopped the black from achieving these rights and resulted in the riots, looting and acts of arson. A good reporter never forgets that the black makes up one-tenth of our country's population and that the men and women of the black community have fought side by side with the white population in every one of our nation's wars from the Revolution to Vietnam.

The following material lists the developments that have brought the black man's demands for equal rights to the forefront of national attention.

1. The 1954 ruling by the U.S. Supreme Court that segregated or "separate but equal" schooling was unconstitutional. The U.S. Department of Justice had to engage in many legal battles just to get, what is considered by many, token school integration. In many Southern cities black children had to be (and still have to be) guarded and supported by police and the Army to gain admission to formerly all white schools.

2. The Montgomery, Alabama bus strike which brought Dr. Martin Luther King, Jr. to national prominence. In December 1955, Mrs. Rosa Parks, a black seamstress, was arrested under a "Jim Crow" law for refusing to give up her bus seat to a white passenger and to move to the back of the bus. A year long boycott by the black men and women of Montgomery brought about a Federal court ruling that prohibited segregated seating on buses.

3. The "sit-in" or nonviolent protest movement that began in Greensboro, North Carolina in 1960, aimed primarily against discrimination at lunch counters, resulted in the Civil Rights Bill of 1964, outlawing segregation and discrimination in public places; placing curbs on job discrimination, and strengthening the black's rights to vote in federal elections.

4. Also, in 1964 Congress passed legislation establishing the Office of Economic Opportunity as part of President Johnson's "Great Society" program, making available billions of dollars for the poor black and white peoples in rural and urban areas.

5. The 1965 law passed by Congress eliminating all legal barriers, such as the poll tax, to black voting rights.

Many whites considered that all this legis
the black man equal with the white and that
were now erased and corrected. But the black
not take the same view. They considered this oi
a first step towards their goal of equal job opp
education, free and easy access to decent
housing, and above all full and complete civil
Added to this was the fact that during this time
mass migration away from the rural areas to t   ...sec-
tions of our country. In fact, since 1950 the black population of
such states as California and Illinois has practically doubled
and New York City has acquired a black population greater
than the entire State of Georgia.

Mutual distrust began to raise its ugly head and a white
backlash ensued. In 1966 Congress voted down a bill which
called for an end to all discrimination in housing; Rev. Martin
Luther King Jr. was stoned and jeered when he led a march
for open housing in Chicago; Father James Groppi, a Roman
Catholic Priest, made headlines in 1967 when many whites
threatened to leave the Catholic Church because he was
leading the Milwaukee protest marches for open housing; and
because white resistance to black violence stiffened the
"black power" movement was born, calling for complete
separatism and preaching hatred for the whites.

Newsmen also should be fully cognizant of the reasons
behind the white man's resistance to the advances of the black
man. They should be knowledgeable of the reports of
sociologists who have been studying this problem. Some of the
reports indicate these findings:

1. The resistance to the black man's advances is based on
prejudice and fear.

2. It is strongest among lower income whites who live in
areas adjacent to the black ghettos. They look upon their
neighborhood as their own private preserve and don't want
their area to become integrated, for to them integration will
result in a complete takeover by the blacks.

3. Whites in the upper or high income bracket fear that
integration will create a dirty, run-down neighborhood with a
proportionate drop in real estate values and the social status
they have attained by living in a certain area.

4. Whites who have "made it" on their own are willing to
agree that blacks are entitled to "equal opportunity" but

...ny contention that the black man is entitled to any help and favoritism.

5. There is a strong feeling that forced integration by busing or any other means will downgrade the education of their children and disrupt their normal pattern of living.

6. Fear that the black will be given special consideration in hiring and job advancement thereby taking over their jobs or positions that they feel they should rightly have.

7. Resentment and anger over some of the statements made by black militants and black extremists.

8. Fear and anger over the increase in the crime rate. They blame the black man for all the muggings, rapes, murders, and robberies and are afraid to walk the streets of the community after nightfall.

9. The large number of blacks, especially women, who are on "relief" while they find it impossible to hire household help.

10. The steady increase of illegitimacy among the blacks on relief.

11. The ingrained belief that whites are superior to blacks and that the black man refuses to help himself by taking advantage of the vast number of projects established to help him.

12. That the "establishment" is too soft on rioters and that the government must stop rewarding a black community where rioting occurs or where violence is preached.

On the other hand, sociologists and black leaders like Bayard Rustin point out that there are many whites who:

1. Deplore this backlash.
2. Contend that the rioting, crime and violence stems from isolation, frustration, and discrimination.
3. Integrated education is necessary to forestall cultural deprivation for both white and black.
4. Deplore the breakdown in dialog between the races.

"Black power" came upon the American scene immediately after James Meredith, the black student who had to have an escort of Federal Marshalls and troops to gain admission to college, was shot and severely wounded allegedly by a white sniper. It gained its impetus when Floyd McKissick, the leader of the Congress of Racial Equality (CORE) and Stokely Carmichael, the leader of the Student Nonviolent Coordinating Committee (SNCC) broke away from the Rev. Martin Luther King Jr. and the NAACP and their "nonviolence" doctrine. In fact both McKissick and Carmichael began to refuse membership, assistance, or aid in any form from white sympathizers. It was they who preached "black power" and disobedience, stating that no black man was bound to obey the laws that were passed by the whites.

Both extremists were criticized and denounced not only by the Rev. Martin Luther King Jr. but also by the white community and such black leaders as Roy Wilkins of the NAACP and Whitney Young of the Urban League. Despite these denouncements both McKissick and Carmichael gained large numbers of followers. Dr. Kenneth Clark, the noted black psychologist states in his book that the reasons behind the popularity of these black extremist leaders is the "tremedous psychological appeal for the masses of negroes with nothing to lose and some middle class negroes who are revolted by empty white promises." The assassinations of the Rev. Martin Luther King Jr. and U.S. Senator Robert Kennedy, who to the vast majority of the black community was their only white champion and hope, has led to a swelling of the ranks among black militant and extremist groups.

THE NEWSMAN AS AN INDIVIDUAL

It is most beneficial for a newsman to have a broad knowledge of the black man's struggle for civil rights, but what about the newsman as an individual. He must realize that, like himself, practically all Americans, white and black alike, have through the legends and tales of the creation and growth of our nation tended to recast our history so as to create a nation above and beyond reality; a nation where the good and the just could always find a refuge against any catastrophe, and that the desire and deep human need for dignity can be satisfied. He must fully comprehend the fact that each new generation of blacks has and will continue to generate their own leaders and visionaries who in the quest for the higher truths will confirm that despite all hostility the black man does have a place in the nation's scheme of things, and that what the black man does or how he behaves are matters of import for everyone in the nation be he white, black, yellow or red.

The good reporter who understands this can emerge as a great reporter. He sees the fallacy in the statement that people are bored and tired of hearing the stories about the plight of the black man. He knows that by his honest reporting he has the power to arouse people and can raise them from their lethargy. He knows that he isn't a teacher, educator, or lecturer but a reporter relating stories of fact and importance. He must shun "literary license." He is not an author or novelist who tells himself that "some events do take place but are not true; other events are true, though they never took place." The novelist's aim as a writer is to pierce the meaning of an experience and transform it into a legend. The reporter's aim is to witness and relate in such a manner as to impart knowledge. He must have the thorough conviction that he is free to choose his own individual attitude in any given situation and have the ability to detach himself from any situation even from himself. The more he follows the dictates of his conscience the greater will be his output, achievement, and accomplishment.

Robert M. Hutchins once stated: "the reason we are headed for the everlasting bonfire is that we have no critical aparatus that can be continuously brought to bear upon the aims and conduct of our society." It is my whole-hearted belief that we do have such an instrument in our free press. Honest, factual, realistic, truthful reports by knowledgeable, unbiased, and concerned newsmen can be the apparatus that will quench the fires of distrust and unrest that are blazing in the ghettos of our nation's minorities.

But what of the reporter as an individual. He must without exception be free from any feeling of bigotry and prejudice. Neither by action or word of mouth should he ever find himself in a position where he can be accused of any act, overt or otherwise, of discrimination, bias, prejudice or bigotry. His conduct and actions must be exemplary in and away from the studio or newsroom, whether on assignment or not. As thinking human beings, reporters naturally have their individual thoughts concerning the nation's racial problems, especially those within his own community. But, regardless of what these private thoughts and opinions may be, he must never allow them to seep into or become apparent in his news reporting. He must condition himself to the fact that there are words, phrases, accents, inflections, gestures, and jokes that are offensive to certain minority groups. His participation in any circumstance or manner, whether active or passive, to any activity abhorent to a minority group can make him suspect and destroy all the trust and reputation a lifetime of work has enabled him to build. As a newsman he should be totally familiar with what these phrases, actions, words, etc., are and should not only avoid their use but shun the company of anyone who makes it a habit to use them.

LANGUAGE

For many years, after a long and courageous fight by the NAACP, the enlightened press of the nation stopped using the word negro as part of their description unless the mention of color was necessary to the story. Today the minorities are demanding that the same consideration be given in describing geographical locations. They frown upon the use of such phrases as "Little Italy," "Hunckeytown," "Harlem's Black Belt," etc., in describing locations. To avoid such usage newsmen today are giving exact house numbers and street names in their reports. They no longer say "in upper Harlem" but rather "on West 145th Street." When a very large area is involved and when it is necessary to the story they will, however, say "The Bedford-Stuyvesant area," or "Harlem's Spanish-Speaking Area." In the first instance, it is to indicate a very large area that has many ethnic groups residing in it even though the majority are "black." In the second instance, it is to dispel the common belief that everyone living in Harlem is "black." Unless there is some relevant racial value in geographical identification all locations should be specifically named by street and city.

All good reporters know that there is a great difference between a "slum" and a "ghetto." Slums are created by people. Ghettos are created by society. A person with the means and the desire can move out of a slum whereas a ghetto dweller is usually confined to that area regardless of his means or desire. Police and law enforcement officials know and have constantly reported that better than 90 percent of all crimes committed in the ghettos are by ghetto dwellers against ghetto dwellers. It is incumbent upon all newsmen to remember this and not to assume under any circumstances that any crime, fire, disturbance, etc., which might occur in a ghetto has racial overtones. Unless circumstances such as curfews or martial law warrant it newsmen should refrain from using the noun "ghetto" as an adjective. This same admonition applies to the noun "negro." Never call an incident a "negro riot" or a "ghetto uprising." It is a riot or an uprising taking place at a specific location and should be so described.

The police today are accused by the extremists of acting only to protect the "establishment." Clashes between the police and extremist groups have been frequent and brought about the use of a much abused phrase "police brutality." In reporting about incidents involving the police and large groups, minority or otherwise, it is imperative that newsmen ferret out both sides of the argument. In issuing statements by police officials or spokesmen for the group involved in an incident be sure to follow the rule of reporting the name of the individual giving or making the statement. If they ask that these names be withheld don't broadcast the statement. Reports relating to "police brutality" should never be broadcast unless the person making the charge is named. Police reports concerning the quilt of any individual should not be broadcast unless the police official is identified. In addition, efforts should be made to ascertain whether the accused has actually admitted his guilt, denied his guilt or, as is his right under the law, remained silent about the charges.

The correct usage of language in describing incidents or demonstrations is most important. Some peaceful demonstrations can become very noisy and disorganized. Very minor clashes, either verbal or physical, may occur either between dissenting groups, between onlookers and the demonstrators, or even within the group of demonstrators. Be very careful about the use of the word "violence." Not every fight or argument is an act that requires the use of the word "violence." Pushing and shoving, name calling, and even the throwing of some missiles should be so described and not referred to as "violence." On the other hand, should violence erupt be sure to so report it giving a full description of the acts involved. Good reporting makes it mandatory that the actions and statements of both sides of any conflict be reported. Don't make the mistake of using only the statements or releases issued by one side. Seek out the opposition and after ascertaining the facts report only the factual. Many veteran newsmen employ the technique of reporting the facts followed by a statement made by the opposition to refute the story. In this way they cannot be accused of showing favortism to any one group.

RAPPORT

The FCC by its rules and regulations makes it mandatory that broadcast licensees seek out and personally interview interested people in the community concerning a radio or television station's program format. This must be done on the broadest level possible. Perhaps because of this the air waves today are presenting more documentaries and programs concerning minority groups than at any time since the beginning of the media. In order to do this the management of a broadcast facility has become familiar with all those who can be labeled as leaders of the minority groups and spokesmen for that section of the population often referred to as underprivileged. In today's age of decentralization a myriad of anti-poverty agencies and organizations and civil rights groups have appeared upon the scene, all making demands and in most cases all looking for exposure and recognition. They look primarily to the mass media for this exposure. They are generally in the forefront of those who are most critical of the manner in which they claim the mass media is mishandling the news.

Practically every state and city in our nation today has some form of a "human rights commission." It is incumbent upon the newsman to know every member of such a commission and through the commission to obtain the names and backgrounds of the leadership of local anti-poverty and minority groups. We all know about such organizations as the NAACP, the Urban League, CORE, SNCC, ADL, etc., but it is necessary for the newsman who aspires to excellence to also know about   ACTION, the Black Panthers, the Black Muslems, Vista, etc. Not only must he know all about such local organizations but must be on speaking terms with each organization's leaders. It is through these contacts that he will be in a position to make proper evaluations of news events. The proper rapport must be created so that these leaders will feel free to offer information and to help the newsman in his evaluations. Therefore, by his contacts he will be able to evaluate the character and leadership ability of these spokesmen, their specific aims, and how they are planning to attain these goals.

It goes without question, of course, that the newsman will also seek to create the same atmosphere with the police, administration officials, leaders of the local chamber of commerce and trade groups, labor and union leaders, churchmen, and leaders of social welfare and civic organizations such as the YMCA, The Red Cross, The Community Chest, Family Service Agencies, Mental Health Groups, Service Clubs, etc. With this knowledge at his fingertips the newsman will be in the enviable position where he can properly evaluate, sift and report on any story that may have racial overtones. He will be able to check out each story with the proper source and will know what stories to release and what stories or rumors have no basis in fact. Let me give you some specific examples of what can be done by citing a few incidents that occurred in the City of Danbury, Connecticut.

The news department of the local radio station received word that the police were called to quell a riot at the local high school. The newsman assigned to cover the story, after checking with the police, arrived at the high school and learned that a serious fight had taken place between two large groups: an all black group of youngsters and an all white group of the school's football team. Two youngsters were hospitalized, one with a knife wound and one with a broken jaw. Because this is a relatively small community and because the police has arrived in mass with sirens blaring many people were aware that something of importance was taking place and the telephones of the police department, newspaper and radio station lit up like Christmas trees. The first report the radio station broadcast, after fully checking with police officials and the newsman at the scene was to advise the listeners that police had been sent to quell a fight between youngsters and that peace and quiet had been restored. The next report indicated that the fight involved a large number of students and that two boys were hospitalized, neither of them were in serious condition. The newscast also informed the listeners that no arrests had been made and that school and police authorities were making further investigations concerning the cause and those who participated in the disturbance.

Because this was a fight between two factions, one all black and the other all white, the newsman immediately contacted the leadership of the black community, especially the leadership of the "Young Afro American Club," to determine whether or not there were any racial implications. As a result of his rapport with these groups the newsman knew that what was told him was the truth and that this was not an incident with racial overtones. He then proceeded to contact the school's athletic director and from him learned the story as told by the football players involved. A young black student had taunted one of the football players on the team's courage in losing the previous Saturday's game. A fist fight ensued and soon others broke out. Before long over 30 boys were engaged in a mass fight. Someone told the police that a riot was taking place and the rest is as reported. Throughout the coverage and broadcasting of this incident the radio station refrained from mentioning at any time that this was a fight between white and black students and made it a point to emphasize that the incident did not have any racial overtones.

A certain section of Danbury became the scene of several sniping incidents. For a period of over three weeks police were called out to investigate reports of automobiles whose windows were pierced by bullets fired by an unknown person. At the request of the police department both the newspaper and the radio station did not report these incidents. It was only when the auto of the Mayor's brother was fired upon while driving home from work that rumors began to fly. In the meantime the radio station's news department was constantly checking with the leadership of the minority groups in the city and from these reliable sources knew that this was not the action of any militant group. In giving its news account the radio station was able to inform the listeners about the fact and to quell any fears or panic. Several weeks later the sniper, a mentally ill white man, was apprehended.

During the early hours of a Sunday morning an incident errupted in Danbury between a very large group of black people and those of the Spanish speaking community. It took all of the efforts of the police, the mayor, and the leadership of both groups before the fighting was brought to a halt. Here again the local radio station was able to properly inform its listeners that this was not a "race riot," although racial implications were present. It was a fight between two social factions and not black against white. The radio station was able to make this determination because its newsmen knew who to contact and who could be relied upon to speak for the minority groups involved.

I could go on citing case after case where improper reporting resulted in false impressions. The improper reporting of a rubbish fire resulted in reports on the national networks that the City of Bridgeport was in the throes of a race riot. Connecticut State Police authorities were very critical when radio and television stations in the City of Hartford improperly reported that riots had broken out in the north end of that city when in fact just a few store windows were broken by a small group of pranksters. The above examples were given to impress upon newsmen and newscasters the importance of fully checking each report and story and that unless he knows where and whom to check he cannot give a proper or adequate report.

I cannot stress too strongly the importance of quoting the source regarding any allegations or charges. But, when doing so the newsman must be absolutely sure that the quote is not only correct but is not given out of context. Here is where the use of the tape recorder can be most helpful. If the report or comment cannot be recorded it would be most helpful to try to

93

every effort should be made to check with the individual before releasing such statements. If it is impossible to contact the individual then the source should be identified when releasing the statement. A newsman should never release the statement if the source refuses to be identified. In releasing statements all newsmen should be aware of the fact that politicians, leaders of minority groups, etc., have for centuries criticized the news media on the ground that they have been misquoted, or that the quote is out of context, or that the press is only using the sensational or controversial part of the statement while withholding the positive aspects of the report or remarks. In checking a statement with an individual, a newsman should be sure to tell the individual the source that ascribed the statement to him. Failure to do this may lead the individual to think of accusing the newsman of originating the story himself.

A legitimate criticism leveled against the news media by the leaders of minority groups charges that the press gives prominence to the arrest of a member of their group but seldom reports when such a person is acquitted. They feel, and rightfully so, that if the news media reports an arrest, the report of an acquittal should receive equal prominence. Newspapers are prime targets for such criticism. The apprehension or arrest is featured on the front page. The acquittal, if reported, is buried somewhere on page 36. The written press has its problems in dealing with this matter.

Radio and television news departments should be able to solve this problem without too much trouble. If an arrest is reported on the 8 AM, 6 PM, or 11 PM newscast, the acquittal should also be reported on the newscast that falls within the same time period. Because of the long delays in getting cases adjudicated, many cases or reported arrests are never followed to the end of the trial. These are several guidelines newsmen should follow when reporting arrests, especially of members of a minority group.

1. Never report an arrest unless it is newsworthy. Family squabbles, unless someone is seriously injured, resulting in a "breach of the peace" arrest is not necessarily a worthy news item. The arrest of a black teenager for shoplifting a dollar item is certainly not newsworthy.

2. Check with the police and give the exact charge as listed on the police blotter in layman's language, but be sure that you cite your cource of information.

3. Try to contact the accused individual or his lawyer for a statement.

4. Advise the individual, his family, or his attorney that you would welcome being kept informed about the progress of the case and that you will report the outcome if they will advise you of it, and that in case of an acquittal you will give it the same prominence that you gave the arrest story.

When riots, disturbances, or incidents involving minority groups do occur, newsmen should be very careful no to rush pell-mell into the situation and give a blow-by-blow description of the event. Nothing whatsoever should be broadcast during the first moments of a developing civil disorder. Give the police and authorities time and the opportunity to quell the disturbance. A premature broadcast of a developing situation can exacerbate the situation. Large crowds can be drawn into the area, thus hindering the work of authorities and adding to the confusion.

When you do begin to broadcast a story of the event, be sure that only verified, and I stress verified, information is given in the calmest and most objective manner possible. Never report the trivial or isolated incidents and be sure to keep the listener informed as to all the steps that are being taken to restore order.

Never assume anything or broadcast conjectures made by anyone. Be sure to cite all sources of information and do not quote out of context. Be careful of your choice of words; remember that an event is not an incident, an incident is not necessarily a disturbance, and a disturbance is not a riot. Until any incident is under control, try to avoid giving the exact location of the disturbance. And, by all means, be sure to constantly advise your listeners to stay away from the area.

When reporting from the scene of the disturbance, try to avoid displaying your call letters or your equipment. A radio microphone too often acts like a magnet and draws all the riff raff and trouble makers. Try to avoid broadcasting the sounds of screaming or fighting or other violence and never, never allow the looter, inciter, or other lawbreaker to gain the use of the microphone.

No set of rules or guidelines can ever be expected to be the catholicon or the entire answer as to the relationship of the mass news media with minority groups. The problems are many and the methods now used and suggested will have to be constantly improved upon and changed. Each individual newsman and each individual news outlet must at all times exercise judgment as each situation arises in their working operations with minority groups and communities. What we in broadcasting must strive for is the highest possible standard of excellence with the best available staff of news gatherers, news reporters, and newscasters that will benefit the entire population and improve the replationships between the races.

Synonyms for Much Used Words

A

ABANDON: desert; forsake; quit
ABATE: wave; decrease; relax
ABDICATE: renounce; resign
ABET: incite; sanction; help
ABHOR: hate; dislike; loathe; detest
ABIDE: continue; stay; remain; dwell
ABJECT: miserable; wretched; base
ABOLISH: annul; abrogate; rescind; revoke; repeal
ABOVE: higher; overhead; up; superior to; in excess of; more than
ABRUPT: sudden; hasty; unexpected
ABSENT: away; lacking; avoid; evade
ABSOLVE: acquit; exonerate; pardon
ABSTAIN: refrain; spare; avoid; be aloof
ABSURD: silly; foolish; ridiculous; proposterous
ABUSE: mistreat; revile; injure; wrong
ACCENT: emphasize; stress; pronounced
ACCEPT: receive; approve; agree to; acquiesce in; consent to
ACCIDENT: mishap; collision; unforseen event
ACCLAIM: praise; kudo; esteem; laud; cheer
ACCOMPLICE: associate; partner in crime
ACCUSE: blame; indict; charge
ACKNOWLEDGE: admit; avow; confess
ACQUIT: exonerate; pardon; absolve
ACTIVE: energetic; vigorous; agile
ACUTE: critical; crucial; sharp
ADAMANT: inflexible; unyielding; firm
ADAPT: adjust; accommodate; conform
ADJACENT: adjoining; contiguous; neighboring
ADJOURN: dissolve; postpone; suspend
ADJUST: adapt; conform; accommodate
ADORE: worship; idolize; revere
ADVERSE: hostile; opposed; harmful
ADVICE: opinion; counsel; information

ADVISE: recommend; notify; inform
AFFECT: influence; impress; sway
AFFIRM: assert; ratify; declare
AFFLICTION: trial; tribulation; misfortune
AFRAID: frightened; timid; fearful
AFTERMATH: result; consequence
AGED: old; senior citizens
AGENT: proxy; deputy; spy
AGILE: nimble; spry; quick
AGITATOR: instigator; inciter; provoker; fomenter
AGONY: pain; distress; grief
AID: help; assistance; subsidy
ALIEN: opposed; unrelated; extraneous
ALIVE: attentive; vigilant; aware
ALLEGE: pretend; adduce; assert
ALLIED: related; similar; like
ALLOW: permit; concede; give
ALLY: confederate; associate; colleague
AMIABLE: friendly; pleasant; hospitable
AMNESTY: forgiveness; pardon
AMPLE: full; large; spacious; plenty; satisfactory
ANARCHIST: radical; revolutionist; destroyer
ANCILLARY: additional; helpful; et cetera
ANTAGONIST: enemy; opponent; adversary; assailant
ANTAGONISTIC: hostile; belligerent; disagreeable; contrary
ANTICIPATE: foresee; expert; preclude
ANTITHESIS: opposite; contrary; difference
APOLOGIZE: defend; justify; excuse; atone
APPALLED: horrified; dismayed; shocked
APPEAR: seem like; manifest; arrive
APPLAUD: cheer; acclaim; sanction; clap; admire
APPRAISE: measure; assess; rate; value
APPROVE: ratify; consent; accept
ARBITRARY: dogmatic; capricious; willful; severe
ARDENT: fervent; zealous; violent
ARGUE: dispute; evince; debate
ARMED: equipped; prepared; mobilized
AROUSE: incite; excite; anger
ARRAY: throng; army; series
ARTFUL: shrewd; cunning; crafty; deceit
ARTISAN: mechanic; craftsman
ASCEND: fly; rise; improve
ASCERTAIN: decide; learn; prove
ASK: inquire; request; invite
ASSIMILATE: adapt; absorb; make alike
ASSOCIATE: ally; confederate; comrade

ASSUMED: supposed; alleged; believed
ASSURE: convince; promise; guarantee
ASTOUND: astonish; amaze; apall; horrify
ASTUTE: sagacious; cunning; artful; crafty
ATOMIZE: shatter; disintegrate; pulverize; vaporize
ATONEMENT: restitution; reparation; expiation
ATROCIOUS: terrible; cruel; wicked; infamous; evil
ATTEND: listen; heed; serve; help; escort
ATTENTIVE: courteous; considerate; respectful
ATTRACTIVE: alluring; beautiful; desirable
AUDACIOUS: defiant; insolent; daring; foolhardy
AUDITION: interview; try out; hearing; examination
AUSPICES: patronage; supervision; protection
AUSTERITY: harshness; severity; economy
AUTHENTIC: genuine; authoritative; confirmed; ratified
AUTHORIZE: commission; sanction; legitimatize
AUTOMATIC: instinctive; involuntary
AVERSION: hatred; unwillingness; repugnance
AVOID: snub; shun; abstain
AVOW: promise; allege; vouch; confess
AWKWARD: embarrassing; clumsy; unwieldy; inelegant
AXIS: center; axle; alliance

B

BACKER: supporter; financier
BACKLOG: reserves; store; fount
BACKSLIDER: recidivist; apostate; recanter; deserter
BAD: evil; nasty; spoiled; wicked; malodorous
BAFFLED: disappointed; perplexed; puzzled
BAIT: lure; snare; trap; harass
BALD: hairless; bare; unadorned
BALM: pacify; calm; relieve
BANDIT: thief; thug; goon; larcenist
BANKRUPT: insolvent; ruin; impoverish
BANQUET: fete; festival; feast
BAR: exclude; prohibit; hinder; close
BARBAROUS: cruel; savage; uncivilized
BARE: bald; naked; exposed; unadorned; disclose
BARGAIN: cheap; negotiate; haggle
BASTARD: scoundrel; illegitimate; false
BATCH: bunch; accumulation; lump
BATTLE: fight; struggle; contend; contest; quarrel
BEAK: nose; spout; prow
BEAR: wear; carry; endure
BECLOUD: conceal; darken; hide

BEFOG: dim; conceal; cloud
BEGUILE: deceive; amuse; fascinate
BELIEVABLE: credible; reliable; unquestionable
BENEVOLENCE: altruism; generosity; kindness
BESET: harass; haunt; worry; persecute
BESPEAK: mean; evince; indicate
BETOKEN: indicate; mean; predict
BETRAY: deceive; divulge; disclose
BEWILDER: astonish; perplex; fluster; confuse
BEWITCH: allure; delight; fascinate; enamor
BICKER: quarrel; argue; quibble; contend
BIDE: wait; endure; tarry
BIGHEARTED: generous; magnanimous; benevolent
BIGOT: fanatic; opinionated; intolerant; biased
BIND: fasten; shackle; obligate
BITTER: caustic; hostile; sour; acrid; unpleasant
BLACKEN: defame; stigmatize; stain; soil
BLAME: attribute; accuse; censure
BLANK: dull; vacant; expressionless
BLASE: unconcerned; nonchalant; disillusioned
BLATANT: noisy; vociferous
BLAZE: fire; light; flash; burn
BLESS: glorify; praise; thank; sanctify
BLOCK: obstruct; hinder; clog
BLOWOUT: feast; party; festival
BLUSTER: agitate; brag; swagger; defy; boast
BOIL: seethe; fume; anger; excite
BOLD: immodest; impudent; courageous; defiant
BONA FIDE: genuine; real; faithful
BOOMERANG: backfire; backlash; recoil
BOOST: assist; lift; push
BOUNDER: scoundrel; upstart; vulgarian
BRASH: gruff; rash; impudent
BRAVADO: defiance; daring; bluster; braggadocio
BREAKDOWN: impairment; failure; debacle
BREWING: imminent; being prepared
BRIEF: short; concise; tacit; terse
BRIEFING: instructing; outlining; summarizing; reporting
BRIGHT: smart; alert; intelligent; colorful; cheerful; optomistic
BROACH: propose; inaugurate; open
BROAD: spacious; extensive; large; wide
BROADCAST: publicize; disperse; publish
BROMIDE: cliche; platitude; banality
BROTHERHOOD: fellowship; kinship; alliance
BRUISE: abuse; beat; wound; buffet
BRUTALITY: cruelty; ruthlessness; barbarism

BUFFET: abuse; bruise; whip; chastise
BULKY: massive; thick; substantial
BULLETIN: message; record; periodical; newsletter
BULWARK: buttress; barrier; fortification; protection
BUM: vagabond; idler; beggar; wretch; drunkard
BUNCH: quantity; multitude; group; flock
BUNK: nonsense; humbug; bombast
BURDEN: hamper; impede; load; weighdown
BURN: anger; annoy; excite; fervor; zeal; blaze
BURST: explode; erupt; emerge; sprout
BURY: conceal; inter; submerge
BUSTLE: activity; excitement; haste; bluster
BYSTANDER: witness; spectator; observer; onlooker

C

CABARET: night club; barroom; inn
CAD: scoundrel; vulgarian; plebeian
CADENCE: rhythm; meter; measure
CAGEY: cunning; wary; evasive
CALAMITY: misfortune; fatality; disaster
CALCULATE: judge; think; suppose; compute
CALCULATING: scheming; judicious; premeditated
CALENDAR: chronology; schedule; log; chronicle
CALL: shout, phone; bid; appeal; invite; visit; demand; challenge
CALL FORTH: elicit; summon; prompt
CALL IN: invite; consult; recall
CALL OFF: end; stop; halt; enumerate
CALL TO MIND: remember; cite; visualize
CALL UPON: urge; petition; beseech; command; visit
CALLOUS: hard; unfeeling; wicked
CALM: composed; quiet; still; peaceful
CALUMNY: insult; slander; malediction
CAMPAIGN: electioneer; journey; expedition
CANCEL: repeal; obliterate; excise
CANDIDATE: aspirant; applicant; nominee
CANNIBAL: man eater; killer; savage; animal; pervert
CANNY: shrewd; cunning; cautious; thrifty
CANVAS: tent; sail; picture; cover; solicit
CAPABLE: able; competent; qualified
CAPACITY: ability; skill; size; character
CAPITALIST: rich man; financier
CAPRICIOUS: irregular; whimsical; changeable
CAPSULE: seedcase; summary; condensation

CAPTIVATE: bewitch; delight; enamor; fascinate
CAPTURE: arrest; seize; catch; imprison; subjudate
CARAVAN: procession; march
CAREFUL: attentive; cautious; heedful; thrifty
CARELESS: slovenly; negligent; impulsive; bungle; reckless; unconcerned
CARESS: fondle; touch; stroke
CARICATURE: picture; exaggeration; burlesque
CAROUSE: revel; dissipate; make merry; tipple
CARRIAGE: posture; mien; behavior
CARRY: transport; extend; support; wear; escort
CARRY AWAY: remove; abduct; fascinate; enamor; delight
CARRY ON: endure; continue; operate; frolic; misbehave; rage; be violent
CARRY OUT: accomplish; execute; apply
CARVE: sever; apportion; sculpture; engrave
CAST: throw; toss; eject; mold; form; color; appearance; roll; quess; calculate
CAST A SLUR ON: stigmatize; censure; libel; slander; accuse
CASUAL: incidental; chance; extemperaneous; informal; nonchalant; haphazard; indiscriminate
CASUALTY: fatality; accident; disaster; calamity
CAUSE: source; principle, motive
CAVE IN: collapse; weaken; yield
CEASE: end; discontinue; disappear
CEASELESS: continuous; perpetual; constant
CEDE: surrender; relinquish; assign
CELEBRATE: glorify; commemorate; praise; rejoice; revel
CELL: prison; compartment; unit
CENSOR: critic; faultfinder; disparager
CENSURE: condemn; expurgate; criticize
CEREMONY: function; ritual; formality
CERTAIN: guaranteed; sure; inevitable; positive; also some and special (certain people)
CHAGRIN: humiliation; mortification
CHALLENGE: defy; protest; confront; doubt
CHAMPION: supporter; patron; defender; best; expert; supreme
CHANCE: possibility; liable; opportunity; probability; risk; gamble
CHANGE: alter; substitute; remove; trade
CHANGEABLE: fickle; capricious; inconsistent; irregular; alterable
CHANNEL: trench; conduit; outlet; frequency; convey
CHARACTER: eccentric; oddball; pecularity; temperment; habit; moral strength
CHARACTERIZE: name; describe; represent
CHARGE: price; commission; fee; attack; accuse; burden; impose; advise; command

CHARM: fascinate; delight; enamor; bewitch; entice; spell talisman; ornament; allure; beauty; sex appeal

CHART: list; diagram; map

CHASE: race; pursuit, pursue; speed; hasten; woo; court

CHASTE: pure; elegant; uncorrupt; tasteful

CHASTEN: punish; restrain; moderate

CHAT: gossip; converse; chatter; conversation

CHATTER: gossip; prattle; shiver; twitter

CHEAP: inexpensive; paltry; niggardly

CHEAT: imposter; sham; deceive; swindle; elude

CHECK: count; measure; test; examine; verify; stop; retard; hinder; curb; restrain; defeat

CHECK IN: arrive; register

CHECK OUT: leave; die

CHECKMATE: defeat; hinder; curb

CHEER: pleasure; conviviality; applause; applaud; regale; gladden; rejoice

CHEERFUL: gay; happy; auspicious; willing; hopeful

CHEERLESS: depressing; unhappy

CHICKEN: coward; mollycoddle; weakling

CHIEF: ruler; principal; main; supreme; top; first; most important

CHILD: urchin; offspring; youth; innocent; unsophisticate

CHILL: refrigerate; discourage; deter

CHOKE: clog; stifle; muffle; strangle; hinder; silence; suppress; extinguish

CHOOSY: selective; particular

CHRISTIAN: respectable; pious; orthodox; human (relating to those of that religious persuasion)

CHRONICLE: account; record; history; analysis

CIRCUIT: lap; tour; cycle; route; sphere

CIRCUMSPECT: judicious; careful; cautious

CIRCUMSTANTIAL: verify; itemize

CIRCUMVENT: deceive; outwit; evade; thwart

CITE: honor; name; summon

CLAIM: pretext; demand; exact; allege

CLAMOROUS: noisy; vociferous; excited; insistent; urgent

CLANNISH: racial; cliquish; exclusive; partisan

CLAPTRAP: nonsense; humbug; trumpery

CLARIFICATION: refinement; elucidation; explanation

CLARITY: distinctness; intelligibility; purity

CLASH: disaccord; contest; hostility; disagree; collide; contend with; counteract; oppose

CLASP: hold; hug; adhere; seize; grip; embrace

CLASSICAL: elegant; literary; tasteful

CLAUSE: section; proviso; phrase; passage

CLEAN-CUT: distinct; precise; clear

CLEANSE: refine; clean; sanctify
CLEAN SWEEP: revolutionize; evacuate; exterminate
CLEAR: distinct; intelligible; manifestness; discernable
CLEAR UP: explain; solve; complete; open; manifest
CLEVER: smart; witty; excellent; skillful; cunning
CLIMAX: result; consummation; summit; crest; peak; cap; culmination
CLOBBER: strike; beat; defeat
CLOD: dolt; rustic; boor; oaf; clumsy fellow
CLOSE: end; stop; cease; complete; imminent; near; intimate; related; about; faithful; airless; dense; sultry
CLOSELY: narrowly; literally; densely; close
CLOSENESS: likeness; nearness; narrowness; secretive; stinginess; intimacy
CLOUDED: concealed; dark; mottled
CLOUDY: dark; opaque; hazy; obscured
CLUE: indication; hint; sign
COALESCENCE: identification; amalgamation; combination
COALITION: combination; affiliation; alliance
COCKINESS: conceit; impudence
COERCION: violence; compulsion; high-pressure methods; duress
COINCIDE: identical; correspond; concur; agree
COLD: frigid; reserved; indifferent; unfeeling; unsociable; unfriendly; heartless
COLLAPSE: debacle; defeat; failure
COLLECT: assemble; procure
COLLIDE: disagree; clash; contend with
COLLISION: contrariety; counteraction; clash; opposition; contest; hostility; disaccordance
COLLOQUIAL: jargon; slang; vernacular; conversational; informal
COLLUSION: chicanery; conspiracy; deceit; conniving
COLOR: hue; appearance; tone; pretext; qualify; change; falsify; distort; dramatize; embellish
COLORLESS: dreary; dull
COMBATANT: fighter; battler; contestant; competitor; disputant; belligerent; militant
COMBINATION: mixture; union; association; affiliation
COMBINE: mix; unite; join; concur
COME: approach; arrive; appear; volunteer
COMFORT: relief; ease; consolation
COMING: eventual; imminent; approaching; arriving; emerging
COMMENSURATE: corresponding; equal; proportionate
COMMENT: critique; annotation; commentary; discourse; treatise; dissertation; remark; gossip; explanation
COMMERCE: trade; traffic; dealings; business; merchantry
COMMON: mutual; prevalent; usual; frequent; well known; colloquial; prosaic; mediocre; trite; vulgar; plain; plebian

COMMOTION: rumpus; turbulence; agitation; excitement
COMMUNICATE: say; inform; converse; write; correspond
COMPACT: contract; crowded; short; concise
COMPARABLE: relative; approximative; similar; analogous
COMPASSION: pity; sympathy; mercy; commiseration
COMPEL: obsess; prompt; force; motivate
COMPETENCE: ability; skill; qualification; adequacy
COMPETENT: able; adequate; effectual; qualified; capable
COMPLIANCE: conformity; assent; willingness; indulgence; submission; obedience; consent
COMPREHENSION: intelligence; understanding; inclusion
COMPULSION: obsession; necessity; urging; compelling
COMPULSORY: necessary; involuntary; mandatory; compelling
CONCEALED: covered; unknown; obscure; secret; hidden
CONCEDE: acknowledge; confess; consent
CONCEITED: opinionated; foppish; proud; vain; boastful
CONCEIVABLE: believable; possible; imaginable
CONCEIVE: originate; understand; know; suppose; think
CONCERNED: implicated; interested; anxious
CONCESSION: qualification; compromise; acknowledgment; confession; consent
CONCLUDE: end; complete; judge; suppose
CONCLUSION: end; result; completion; judgment; opinion
CONCLUSIVE: final; decisive; mandatory
CONCOCT: invent; make up; devise; prepare
CONCUR: agree; cooperate; coact
CONDEMN: censure; convict; penalize; damn
CONDENSE: intensify; contract; shorten; densify
CONDONE: forgive; tolerate
CONFEDERACY: conspiracy; affiliation; alliance
CONFEDERATE: partner; comrade
CONFERENCE: audition; discussion; parley; council
CONFIDENCE: secret; belief; sureness; poise; hope; courage
CONFIDENT: convinced; sure; poised; hopeful; unafraid
CONFLICT: contrariety; counteraction; opposition; contention; contest; hostility
CONSEQUENCE: effect; influence; deduction; distinction; importance
CONSIDER: think; discuss; examine; judge; suppose
CONSIDERATE: judicious, careful; kind
CONSISTENT: uniform; coherent; consonant
CONSORT: confederate; companion; accomplice; spouse
CONSPICUOUS: remarkable, distinct; obvious, distinguished
CONSTANT: uniform; continuous; durable; perpetual; unchangeable
CONSTRAINT: moderation; reserve; urge; compulsion; restraint; modesty
CONSTRUCTIVE: creative; suggestive; interpretative

CONSUMING: agonizing; engrossing; harrowing
CONTAMINATE: adulterate; defile; infect; corrupt
CONTEMPLATION: thought; examination; expectation; intention
CONTEMPT: defiance; arrogance; disdain; ridicule
CONTEND: argue; maintain; insist; contest; struggle
CONTENTION: argument; question; quarrel; strife
CONTEST: contention; game; argue; deny; oppose; contend; dispute
CONTINUE: endure; protract; postpone; extend; perservere
CONTRADICT: refute; deny; oppose
CONTRARY: opposite; denying; refutive; perverse; adverse; opposed
CONTRAVENE: refute; deny; thwart; violate; oppose
CONTROVERSY: argument; quarrel; contention
CONVENIENT: opportune; nearby; available; comfortable
CONVULSE: agitate; pain; torture; discompose
COOL: calm; refrigerate; ventilate; discourage; level headed; reserved; unfeeling; unfriendly
COOPERATION: collusion; collaboration
COORDINATE: equalize, integrate; harmonize; organize
COPIOUS: abundant; fertile; diffuse
COPY: ape; mimic; imitate; pattern; borrow; transcribe; replica; counterfeit
COQUET: flirt; trifler
CORDIAL: friendly; kind; hospitable; ungrudging; pleasant
CORNER: nook; hiding place; impasse
COROLLARY: deduction; effect; addition
CORPULENT: obese; fat; overweight; stout; bulky
CORRECT: amend; edit; remedy; accurate; right; proper
CORRESPOND: coincide; agree; equal; conform; concur; identical; similar; write
CORRODE: disintegrate; deteriorate; harm; decay; rot
CORRUPT: adulterate; bribe; defile; debase; spoil; impure; wicked; venal; dishonest
COUNCIL: assembly; conference; tribunal
COUNSEL: advise; deliberate; consult; confer
COUNTER: oppose; retaliate; disobey
COUNTERFEIT: sham; affect; false; imitate
COUNTLESS: infinite; innumerable; numerous
COURTLY: dignified; gallant; flattering
COVER: refuge; hiding place; pretext; protect; conceal
COVET: desire; envy; jealousy
CRACK: break; cleft; snap
CRAM: crowd; press; overfill
CRAMP: confine; hamper; restrict
CRANK: monomaniac; eccentric; malcontent; grouch
CRASS: stupid; vulgar
CRAWL: creep; backout; grovel

106

CREATE: produce; invent; originate
CREDITABLE: reputable; honorable; praiseworthy
CRESTFALLEN: dejected; humiliated
CRIMINAL: thief; thug; felon; swindler; malefactor; hoodlum; hooligan; crook; racketeer; outlaw
CRINGE: cower; shrink; grovel; flinch
CRIPPLE: impair; disable; injure
CRISP: concise; cold; brittle; friable
CRITICAL: crucial; urgent; precarious; exacting; discriminating
CRITICIZE: censure; judge; comment upon
CROUCH: stoop; cower; grovel
CROW: exult; laugh
CROWD: throng; mob; group; party; band; gang
CRUDE: raw; vulgar; garish; inelegant
CRUEL: heartless; ruthless; painful
CRUISER: patrol car; prowl car; squad car
CRUMBLE: disintegrate; decay; destroy
CRUSHED: humiliated; wretched; conquered; subdued
CRY: entreat; weep; plaint; howl
CRYPT: tomb; compartment; hiding place
CUE: hint; clue; suggestion
CULTURED: learned; refined; well-bred
CUMBERSOME: bulky; burdensome; unwielding
CUNNING: shrewdness; deceit; trickery; crafty; clever
CURATOR: guardian; manager
CURB: restrain; hinder; retard
CURRENT: prevalent; usual; present; customary
CURSORY: slight; careless; hasty
CURT: short; concise; gruff
CURTAIL: reduce; shorten; deprive; retrench
CUSTOM: tradition; habit
CUSTOMARY: usual; traditional; habitual; conventional
CUT: split; cleft; slice; lash; injure; offense; gibe; reduce; excise; sever; dilute

D

DABBLE: meddle; interfere; intrude; officious
DAINTY: delicate; pleasing; fastidious
DALLY: delay; irresolute; inactive
DAMAGE: injure; spoil; mar; impair; despoil
DAMN: condemn; proscribe; doom
DAMP: moist; cold; depress; dull
DANGER: peril; risk; jeopardy; hazard
DANGLE: hang; swing; display

107

DARE: suppose; defy; challenge; threaten

DARK: obscure; dim; black; blind; invisible; insidious

DATA: evidence; facts; premises

DAZZLE: astonish; awe; blind

DEAD: inert; colorless; lifeless; ended; finished; impotent; useless; ceased

DEADEN: weaken; moderate; mute

DEADLY: unhealthy; killing; pernicious

DEBATE: dispute; reason; talk; converse

DECAY: rot; spoil; decompose

DECEIT: falsehood; cunning; deception; dupe

DECIDE: choose; resolve; judge

DECIMATE: weaken; punish; kill; play havoc

DECISION: resolution; judgment; intention

DECLINE: refuse; reject; decrease; descent

DECOY: lure; entice; tempt

DECREPIT: old; weak; decayed

DEDUCTION: inference; reasoning; conclusion; judgment

DEEP: intense; great; profound

DEFACE: destroy; obliterate; injure; make ugly

DEFEAT: failure; unsuccessful; loss; best; conquered; triumphed over

DEFECTIVE: incomplete; insufficient; imperfect

DEFERENCE: respect; courtesy; obedience

DEFIANCE: dare; challenge; scorn; disobedience; rebellion; insolence

DEFICIENT: inferior; incomplete; imperfect

DEFILE: spoil; dirty; make impure

DEFINE: specify; name; explain

DEFY: disobey; dare; threaten; challenge; rebel

DELAY: defer; postpone; demur; retard; respite; reprieve

DELEGATE: transfer; consign; commission; deputize

DELIBERATE: slow; cautious; think; opine

DELINEATE: describe; outline; represent

DEMAND: inquire; ask; order

DEMEANOR: behavior; carriage; conduct

DEMUR: hesitate; disbelieve; dissent

DENOTE: specify; mean; indicate

DENOUNCE: curse; accuse; disapprove

DENY: dissent; negate; refuse

DEROGATE: underrate; disparage; dishonor; shame

DESECRATE: profane; misuse; disrespect

DESERVE: merit; entitled

DESIGN: intention; plan

DESIST: discontinue; relinquish; cease

DESOLATE: alone; secluded; dejected

DESPICABLE: shameful; contemptible

DESPISE: scorn; condemn; disdain; deride

108

DESPOIL: rob; injure; loot
DESTROY: demolish; injure; subvert; exterminate; ruin; ravage; raze; pulverize
DETECT: find; discover; evolve; trace; unearth
DETERMINE: define; judge; resolve
DETEST: dislike; hate; shun; loathe; abhor
DETRACT: defame; slander; underrate
DEVELOP: increase; produce; expand; evolve
DEVOID: empty; absent
DEVOTEE: zealot; fanatic; aspirant
DICTATE: command; enjoin; advise
DIGNITY: honor; glory; pride
DILATE: increase; widen; swell
DILATORY: slow; inactive
DIP: water; baptize; insert
DIRE: fearful; grievous; disastrous
DIRECTION: precept; indication; tendency
DIRTY: unlean; disreputable; dishonorable; opaque; dim
DISAFFECTION: hate; enmity; dissent
DISAGREEMENT: difference; dissent; discord; incongruity
DISAPPOINT: crush; dash; balk; jilt
DISASTER: calamity; adversity; failure
DISBAND: separate; dispense; liberate
DISCARD: surrender; abrogate; relinquish
DISCHARGE: propel; emit; excrete; complete; liberate; acquit
DISCONCERT: distract; hinder; confuse
DISCORD: dissension; difference; disagreement
DISCOURAGE: sadden; dissuade; frighten
DISCOURSE: sermon; talk; speech
DISCOVER: disclose; find; solve; perceive
DISCRETION: caution; wariness; carefulness; prudence
DISCUSS: dissent; reason; inquire
DISENTANGLE: liberate; separate; unroll; decipher
DISFIGURE: deface; deform; injure; blemish
DISGUISE: conceal; mask; falsify
DISGUST: hatred; dislike; offensive
DISHEARTEN: dissuade; deject; pain
DISHEVEL: untidy; disorder; loose
DISHONOR: disrepute; disrespect; baseness
DISINTEGRATE: separate; decompose; pulverize
DISMISS: discharge; discard; abrogate
DISORDER: confusion; derangement; disarray; chaos; turmoil; pother; row; tumult; uproar; riot
DISORDERLY: irregular; untidy; slovenly; bedraggled; messy; chaotic; unsystematic; unprincipled
DISORGANIZE: derange; destroy; spoil

DISPARAGE: detract; underrate; disrespect
DISPARITY: unequal; disagreeing; different
DISPENSE: disperse; give; apportion
DISPLACE: derange; remove; transfer
DISPUTE: discord; doubt; discuss; deny
DISREGARD: overlook; neglect; contempt; disrespect
DISSEMINATE: scatter; publish; teach
DISSOLVE: vanish; disappear; abrogate
DISTINCT: audible; visible; intelligible; atriculate; manifest
DISTORT: twist; misinterpret; misrepresent
DISTURB: excite; agitate; change; derange
DISUNION: separation; discord; disorder
DIVERGENCE: difference; variation; deviation; disagreement
DIVERSE: different; many; several; multiform
DIVERSION: amusement; pleasure; deviation; change
DIVIDE: separate; disect; apportion
DOCTRINE: dogma; tenet; principle
DODGE: shift; avoid; deviate
DONE: finished; ceased; tired; impotent
DORMANT: inert; latent; asleep
DOUBLECROSS: deception; fraud; deceit; delude; chicanery; treachery; trick; cheat; deceive
DOUBT: unsure; uncertain; skepticism; disbelieve
DOUSE: immerse; splash; extinguish
DOWNFALL: misfortune; failure; destruction
DRAIN: empty; exhaust; dissipate
DRAWBACK: hindrance; imperfection; obstruction; obstacle
DREARY: melancholy; solitary; monotonous
DRIVE: propel; urge; compel
DROP: discard; discontinue; relinquish
DUCTILE: elastic; flexible; easy; docile
DULCET: sweet; melodious; agreeable
DULL: weak; inert; blunt; dim
DUMBFOUND: astonish; amaze; silence
DUPLICATE: imitate; copy; carbon-copy; reproduce; repeat
DWINDLE: abate; lessen; shrink

E

ENDURE: last; persist; continue; feel
ENERGY: power; strength; resolution
ENFORCE: urge; compel; require
ENGAGE: undertake; induce; promise; commission
ENGULF: swallow up; destroy; plunge

ENIGMATIC: obscure; uncertain; unintelligible
ENLIGHTEN: illuminate; inform; teach
ENLIVEN: amuse; cheer; delight
ENRAPTURE: love; beatify; excite
ENTANGLE: embroil; entrap; interlink; derange
ENTENTE: agreement; alliance; friendship
ENTERTAIN: support; bear in mind; amuse
ENTHUSIASTIC: excitable; imaginative; sanguine; sensitive
ENTIRE: all; whole; complete
ENUNCIATE: inform; affirm; voice
EQUITABLE: wise; just; honorable
EQUIVALENT: identical; same; equal; substitute
ERRATIC: irregular; changeable; capricious
ERUPTION: upheaval; violence
ESCHEW: avoid; dislike; disapprove
ESPOUSE: marry; aid; choose; cooperate
ESSENTIAL: important; required; intrinsic
ESTEEM: reputation; approve; believe
ESTIMATE: measure; judge; inform
ETIQUETTE: fashion; custom; ceremony
EVACUATE: quit; emit; excrete
EVEN: uniform; equal; level; flat; smooth
EVENT: circumstance; expectation; happening
EVIDENT: visible; manifest; certain; concrete
EVIL: harm; badness; malevolence
EVINCE: show; prove; disclose
EVOKE: call upon; excite; cause
EXACERBATE: increase; aggravate; exasperate
EXACTING: severe; fastidious; discontented
EXAGGERATE: expand; increase; magnify; misrepresent
EXASPERATE: exacerbate; aggravate; enrage
EXCLUDE: leave out; reject; banish; prohibit
EXCUSE: vindicate; exempt; forgive; plea
EXEMPTION: exception; qualification; permission
EXHAUST: empty; drain; squander; waste; fatigue
EXHIBIT: evidence; show; display
EXIGENCY: crisis; difficulty; need; requirement
EXONERATE: release; forgive; vindicate; acquit
EXORBITANT: redundant; enormous
EXPEDITE: aid; hasten; quicken
EXPOSE: describe; disclose; manifest
EXQUISITE: savory; beautiful; excellent; pleasurable
EXTEMPORANEOUS: instant; unprepared; off-hand
EXTINGUISH: danken; blow out; destroy
EXTORT: extract; despoil; compel
EXTRANEOUS: outside; foreign; not related
EXTRICATE: liberate; facilitate; take out

111

F

FABLE: fiction; false; fib; fabrication
FABRICATE: invent; compose; falsify; lie
FABULOUS: enormous; exaggerated; imaginary
FACE: front; resist; oppose; brave; exterior; covering
FACILE: easy; willing; irresolute
FACT: truth; certainty; existence; event
FACULTY: skill; power; art; ability
FADE: vanish; age; droop; disappear
FAILURE: blunder; mishap; mistake; slip; defeat
FAINT: swoon; dim; weak; impotent
FAIR: pale; white; good; moderate; just; honorable
FALLOW: unproductive; unready; inactive
FALSE: untrue; spurious; counterfeit; dishonorable
FEATURE: component; character; appearance
FEEL: sense; touch; pity
FELLOWSHIP: partnership; friendship; companionship
FELON: sinner; rascal; scoundrel; villain; thief; reprobate; culprit;
ruffian; hoodlum; murderer; criminal; malefactor
FELONIOUS: nefarious; base; sinister; shameful; heinous; scandalous;
grave; fiendish; wrong; sinful
FELONY: misconduct; malpractice; sin; transgression; dereliction;
delinquency; indiscretion; offense; trespass; crime; malefaction
FEMALE: woman; petticoat; fair sex; dame
FERMENT: disorder; violence; agitation; anger
FERVENT: desirous; longing; hot
FERVID: excited; heartfelt; hot
FEUD: discord; disagreement; clash; dissention; quarrel; dispute
FEVER: excitement; restlessness; impatience; hot
FICTION: story; yarn; untruth; falsehood; fabricating; fable; coward;
white lie
FIELD: scope; region; arena
FIEND: oppressor, tyrant; destroyer; terrorist; gangster; racketeer;
brute; ruffian; barbarian; hooligan; desperado; thief
FIERCE: violent; angry; daring
FIERY: violent; hot; excitable; angry; irascible
FIGHT: contention; strife; contest; struggle; oppose; quarrel; rivalry;
fracas; tussle; battle; conflict; skirmish; duel
FILE: reduce; smooth; pulverize; record; store; list; row
FILIBUSTER: delay; defer; postpone; protract; prolong; obstruct;
stop; stay
FILTER: percolate; emerge; leak; seep; trickle

112

FILTH: uncleanness; defilement; contamination; decay; putrescence; slovenly; dirt; slop; smut; grime; offal; garbage; dung
FINAL: ending; completing; conclusive
FINALE: end; conclusion; completion
FIND: acquire; discover; adjudge
FINE: small; thin; rare; exact
FINICAL: trifling; affected; fastidious
FIRE: heat; excite; vigor; enthusiasm; discharge
FIRM: hard; resolute; brave; stable
FLACCID: empty; soft; weak
FLAGRANT: atrocious; notorious; great; manifest
FLAME: fire; light; luminary; passion
FLAMING: violet; excited; ostentatious
FLASH-IN-THE-PAN: unsubstantial; impotent; failure
FLAT: abode; tenement; inert; low; horizontal; dejected; weary; dull
FLATTERY: adulation; blandishment; fawning; praising
FLAUNT: display; show; flourish; parade; strut
FLAW: break; crack; error; imperfection; blemish
FLEECE: strip; rob; impoverish; overcharge
FLIMSY: weak; unsubstantial; trifling; soft
FLOUNDER: toss; bungle; fail; uncertain
FLOURISH: brandish; display; exaggerate; boast; prosper
FLUCTUATE: change; oscillate; irresolute
FLUSHED: excited; cheerful; hopeful; proud; vain
FLY-IN-THE-FACE-OF: oppose; resist; disobey; insolence
FOAM: spray; boil; violent; excitement; froth
FOG: mist; haze; steam; vapor; mask; conceal; veil; cover; screen; becloud
FOLLOW: conform; pursue; ensue; result; cooperate; imitate; continue
FOMENT: stimulate; promote; excite
FONDLE: caress; pet; cuddle; hug; embrace
FONDNESS: desire; wish; fancy; longing; hankering; liking; craving
FOOL: deceive; ridicule; disappoint; flatter; bungler
FORBEAR: avoid; abstain; pity; spare
FORCE: energy; power; strength; violence; urge; exert; compel
FORECAST: prediction; premonition; prophecy; augury; presage; omen; herald; harbinger
FOREGONE: past; prejudged; predetermined
FOREIGN: alien; exotic; irrelative; unrelated; extraneous; strange; remote
FOREMOST: beginning; superior; important; reputed
FOREGO: relinquish; renounce; surrender
FORGOTTEN: past; gone; over; expired; extinct; obsolete; formerly; unrewarded; unthanked; unacknowledged
FORLORN: dejected; hopeless; deserted
FORM: shape; likeness; makeup; arrange; fashion

FORMULA: precept; rule; law; maxim

FORESAKE: relinquish; abandon; desert; vacate; renounce; forego; desist

FORTUITOUS: lucky; extrinsic; undesigned; chance

FORTUNATE: opportune; successful; prosperous; lucky

FORWARD: advance; help; improve; transmit; send; vain; insolent; uncourteous

FOUL: bad; dirty; unhealthy; ugly; base; vicious

FOUNDATION: beginning; inaugural; pillar; base; substructure; support; footing

FRACAS: disorder; contention; discord; noise

FRAIL: weak; feeble; imperfect; brittle; irresolute

FRANK: open; sincere; honest; artless; honorable

FRANTIC: violent; excited; delirious

FRATERNIZE: associate; agree; sympathize; cooperate

FRAUD: falsehood; lie; deception; pretense; pretender

FRAUGHT: full; possessing; pregnant

FREE: detached; unobstructed; unconditional; exempt; liberate; rid; at liberty; gratis; liberal

FREE (and easy): cheerful; adventurous, friendly; sociable

FRENZY: madness; excitement; immagination

FREQUENT: often; repeated; redundant; many; several; unseldom; sometimes; occasionally; visit; haunt

FRESH: new; additional; good; healthy

FRET: suffer; grieve; irritate

FRIVOLOUS: unreasonable; foolish; capricious; trivial

FRONT: foremost; forepast; insolence; resist; surpass

FROWN: lower; scowl; sulk; disapprove

FUGITIVE: transient; refugee; runaway; renegade; deserter; emigrant; truant

FULL: much; complete; large; abundant; active; expanded; strong

FULMINATE: propel; threaten; violent; accuse

FUMBLE: awkward; derange; grope; mishandle

FUNNY: comical; odd; humorous

FURBISH: improve; prepare; adorn

FURIOUS: violent; hasty; passionate; angry

FURNISH: provide; prepare; give; aid

FUROR: passion; desire; emotion

FURY: violence; excitation; anger; demon

FUSE: join; combine; heat

FUSS: activity; agitation; haste; difficulty; excitement; lament; disapprove

FUZZY: dim; obscured; blurred; misty; confused; indefinite; undefined

G

GAB: talk; chatter; mouth
GAG: restrain; silence; shackle
GAIN: acquire; benefit; profit; increase
GALLANT: cavalier; dandy; lover; courageous; courteous
GALLERY: platform; porch; balcony; audience
GAMBLE: risk; chance; uncertainty; rely on
GAME: contest; amusement; courage; pluck
GANG: company; association; society; ring
GANGSTER: thief; criminal; robber; crook; felon; racketeer; desperado; outlaw; lawbreaker
GAPE: yawn; stare; wonder
GARBLE: distort; misinterpret; falsify
GASH: injure; mark; notch; sever
GASSY: boastful; bombastic; pompous; talkative; vaporous
GATE: portal; barrier; receipts
GAY: colorful; cheerful; festive; convivial
GEL: thicken; coagulate; congeal; consolidate
GENERALLY: usually; indefinitely; approximately
GENEROSITY: magnanimity; liberality; hospitality
GENIAL: warm; pleasant; cheerful; amiable; friendly
GENIUS: inspiration; prodigy; talent
GENTEEL: refined; well-bred; well-born
GENTLE: domesticate; tame temperate; lenient; tender; kindly; humane; meek; slow; soft
GENUINE: real; unadulterated; authentic
GERMANE: relative; pertinent; apropos
GET: gain; acquire; receive; incur
GHOUL: fiend; demon; grave-robber
GIBBERISH: nonsense; blather; babble; prattle; dribble
GILD: coat; paint; falsify
GIMMICK: bind; strengthen; prepare; encircle
GIST: essence; meaning; content; mainpoint
GIVE: pliancy; elasticity; inform; provide; bestow; present; administer
GIVE IN: consent; yield; surrender
GIVE OFF: exude; reek; let out; excrete
GLAD: willing; pleased; cheerful
GLAMORIZE: beautify; glorify; charm; bewitch
GLARING: bright; distinct; obvious; garish
GLIB: loquacious; facile; suave; hypocrital
GLIMPSE: glance; peek; wink; casual glance; behold; see; view; witness; catch sight of

GLOAT: exult; glory; delight; crow over
GLOOMINESS: darkness; sadness; pessimism; ominousness
GLORIFY: honor; praise; sanctify; worship
GLORIOUS: superb; magnificent; beautiful; illustrious
GLOWING: burning; luminous; red; eloquent; fervent; enthusiastic; excited; beautiful
GLUT: stuff; satiate; gorge
GO AFTER: fetch; follow; pursue
GO AGAINST: oppose; counteract
GO AHEAD: proceed; improve; begin
GO ALONG WITH: concur; agree; cooperate
GO AWAY: separate; recede; depart; disappear
GO BACK: retreat; recur; revert
GO BACK TO: resume; revert; revisit
GO INTO: enter; begin; develop; discuss; undertake
GO ON: endure; continue; resume; proceed; depart; perservere
GO OVER: reiterate; traverse; examine; read; rehearse
GO WITH: agree; concur; accompany; date
GOAL: end; destruction; objective
GO-BETWEEN: intermediary; mediator; interagent
GODSPEED: leave-taking; parting; adieu; farewell; goodbye
GOLIATH: giant; stalwart; powerhouse; titan; colossus
GONE: past; absent; nonexistent; departed; dead; lost; vanished; forgotten
GOOD: savory; valid; genuine; ample; excellent; pleasant; kind; proper; just; virtuous; benevolent
GOOD FOR: worth; useful; beneficial; helpful; salubrious; solvent; reliable; responsible
GOODLINESS: pleasantness; comeliness; goodness; kindness
GOODWILL: favor; benevolence; charity; philanthropy; altruism; brotherly love; willingness
GORY: blood-red; murderous; bloody
GOSSIP: tattle; newsmonger; rumormonger; scandalmonger; busybody; talebearer; tattletale; blabber
GOVERN: regulate; manage; supervise; rule
GRACE: kindness; clemency; forgiveness; reprieve; tact; elegant style; prayer; sanctification
GRACIOUS: ungrudging; indulgent; hospitable; courteous; kind
GRAND: great; large; important; good; eminent
GRANDEUR: greatness; eloquence; ostentation; dignity
GRANT: gift; subsidy; sanction; right; acknowledge; confess; admit; give; permit; allow for
GRASP: understand; hold; seize; adhere
GRATE: chafe; annoy; grind; pulverize; sound harshly; rack the nerves
GRATEFUL: welcome; thankful; pleasant
GRATIFY: feed; indulge; please; welcome

116

GRAVE: great; important; dignified; dark; due; painful; sad; solemn

GRAZE: touch; sideswipe; abrade; browse

GREAT: grand; large; important; good; famous; chief; drastic; magnanimous

GREED: avarice; cupidity; lust; insatiability; gluttony; piggishness; voracity

GREEN: new; immature; sour; ignorant; undeveloped; inexperienced; unskilled

GREENHORN: dupe; ignoramous; novice

GREET: accost; hail; curtsy; salute

GRIEF: sorrow; remorse; mishap; unfortunate event

GRIEVANCE: evil; bane; affliction; complaint; injustice

GRIEVE: sorrow; lament; distress; offend; pain

GRIM: unyielding; stern; solemn; sullen; harsh; bad; horrible

GRIPE: pain; annoy; complaint; complain

GRIPPED: held; obsessed; interested

GROOVE: routine; track; rut; daily grind; furrow; cut; gash; incision; gouge; slit; chisel

GROSS: very bad; coarse; stupid; absurd; vulgar; infamous; indecent; carnal; inelegant

GROUNDS: basis; attitudes; motives; justification

GROUP: assembly class; company; set; bunch; sect; arrange; assemble; classify; organize

GROVEL: crawl; crouch; wallow; truckle

GROW: increase; enlarge; develop; mature; raise; produce

GRUELING: weakening; exhausting; trying; punishing

GRUESOME: hideous; horrible; frightful; dreadful; terrible; awful; repulsive; repugnant; offensive; ghastly; grisly

GUARD: vigilance; protection; defense; safeguard; precaution; protect; defend; restrain

GUARDED: qualified; vigilant; protected; restrained; cautious

GUESS: conjecture; inference; surmise; think; opine; suppose; assume; presume; judge; suspect; imagine; consider; estimate

GUIDE: director; advisor; teacher; escort; pilot; direct; advise; teach; influence

GUISE: way; mode; appearance; behavior; pretext; cover

GUSTO: savor; liking; fervor; pleasure; eagerness

GUTS: insides; vitals; intestines; stamina; pluck; courage

GYP: racket; swindle; fraud; deceive; trick; cheat; bilk

H

HABIT: nature; custom; mannerism; clothing

HABITUAL: addict; regular; frequent; persistent; recurring

HACKNEYED: trite; corny; banal; common; familiar; stale

HAG: crone; vixen; witch; ugly person

HAGGARD: thin; pale; deathlike; overwrought; tired-looking

HAGGLE: bargain; dicker; negotiate

HAIL: accost; greet; acclaim

HAIRSPLITTING: quibbling; hypercritical; overparticular

HALCYON: auspicious; tranquil; peaceful; pleasant

HALF-BAKED: premature; unprepared; inexperienced; half-cocked

HALT: delay; stop; prevent; standstill; respite; impasse; cease; lag

HAMPER: basket; hinder; restrain; burden; impede

(AT) HAND: imminent; present; nearly

(CAME TO) HAND: arrived; appeared; found; received

(GIVE A) HAND: aid; abet; help; applaud; clap; cheer

(HAVE NO) HAND: avoid; abstain; let alone

(HELPING) HAND: aid; assist; abet; benefactor; assistant

(ON) HAND: present; in stock; in store; handy; possessing

(ON THE OTHER) HAND: contrarily; otherwise; notwithstanding

HAND OVER: transfer; assign; deliver

HANDICAP: impediment; burden; impede; hamper; penalize; equalize

HANDLE: name; title; operate; pilot; touch; use; manage; deal in

HANDSOME: beautiful; generous; magnanimous

HANDY: nearby; convenient; skillful

HANG: droop; suspend; hover

HANG ON: adhere; perservere; hold on; depend on; attribute to; be absorbed

HANGOUT: haunt; nest; den; stamping grounds; meeting place

HANKERING: longing; yearning; pining; desire; wish; urge; liking; fondness; passion; suppressed desire

HAPHAZARD: slipshod; slovenly; clumsy; hit or miss; careless; random

HAPPENING: event; occurrence; incident; episode; occasion; affair; prevalent; current; chance event; accident

HAPPILY: gladly; cheerfully; willingly; auspiciously

HAPPY: auspicious; joyful; cheerful; timely; apt

HARASS: persecute; torment; worry; bully; fatigue; annoy

HARBINGER: forerunner; precursor; omen; foretoken; messenger; herald; portent; augury; sign; token; intimation; indication; foreshadowing

HARD: strong; rigid; painful; bitter; obstinate; difficult; strict; callous; harsh; heartless

HARDENED: indurate; inveterate; impenitent; wicked

HARDHEADED: sagacious; ungullible; obstinate; strict

HARDLY: scarcely; unusually; infrequently

HARDY: strong; perennial; healthy; courageous

HARM: injure; damage; disadvantage; evil; impairment

HARMONIOUS: agreeing; orderly, in accord; attuned; organized; in conformity; symmetry; accord

HARPY: fiend; plunderer; extortionist

HARRY: persecute; besiege; harass; worry

HARSH: acrimonious; severe; gruff; unkind; painful; bitter; pungent; inelegant; raucous

HASH: jumble; failure; bungle; botch; spoil; shatter

HASTEN: speed; urge; hurry; further; facilitate

HASTILY: prematurely; swiftly; impulsively; hurriedly; recklessly

HASTY: sudden; premature; speedy; impulsive; hurried; reckless; hot-tempered

HATCH: invent; generate; plot; trump up

HATE: dislike; detest; loathe; abhor; aversion; antipathy; odium; malice

HATEFUL: terrible; odious; malicious

(THE) HAVES: the rich; the wealthy; plutocracy; timocracy

HAVOC: harm; devastation; botch; spoil

HAZARD: chance; gamble; danger; presume

HAZINESS: dimness; opaqueness; cloudiness; indistinctness; vagueness

HAZY: muddled; obscure; indistinct; dim; opaque; cloudy; vague

HEAD UP: precede; begin; caption; direct; govern; front; first; top

HEADFIRST: recklessly; hastily; carelessly; impetuously

HEADING: top; front; direction; precession; topic; caption

HEADLINE: title; caption; feature; star; dramatize; banner; streamer; spread

HEADLONG: impulsive; hasty; reckless; sudden

HEAP: quantity; throng; large amount; pile; load; exaggerate; save; give; broken down auto

HEAR: listen; judge; learn; consent; permit

HEARING: audition; tryout; interview; examination; scolding; trial

HEARSAY: rumor; report; rumble; common talk; scuttlebutt; canard

HEART: essence; substance; center; vitals; meat; courage; emotion

HEAT: cook; hotness; fever; fervor; excitement; passion; violence; anger

HEAVE: throw; toss; pull; lift; billow

HEAVENLY: celestial; delightful; beautiful; divine; angelic; sacred; godly

HEAVY: substantial; great; thick; steep; inert; weighty; dense; viscid; important; difficult; dull; languid

HECKLER: tormentor; pest; tease; annoyer; harasser; harrier; badgerer; persecutor; bully

HECTIC: reddened; feverish; excited

HEED: listen; attend; care; obey; observe; caution; consider

HEEDLESS: incurious; inattentive; careless; impulsive; unconcerned; inconsiderate; improvident

HEIGHTEN: intensify; raise; exaggerate; aggravate

HEINOUS: terrible; infamous; wicked

(RAISE) HELL: create a disturbance; vociferate; be noisy; cause trouble

HELLCAT: violent person; daredevil; hellion; mischief maker

HELLISH: execrable; cruel; wicked; infernal; devilish

HELP: aid; abet; assist; remedy; subsidy; servant; assistant; benefactor; benefit

HELPFUL: instrumental; useful; beneficial

HELPLESS: impotent; unprotected; forlorn; defenseless

HELTER-SKELTER: confusion; haste; in disorder; recklessly; carelessly

HEM: surround; border; enclose; confine; stammer; vacillate

HENCHMAN: follower; tagtail; attendant; adherent; partisan; hanger-on

HERALD: forerunner; harbinger; messengers; presage; proclaim

HERCULEAN: strong; gigantic; difficult; laborious

HERE AND THERE: intermittently; scatteringly; sparsely

HERO: victor; brave man; ace; celebrity; demigod

HESITANT: uncertain; unwilling; irresolute

HESITATE: procrastinate; pause; demur; stammer; irresolute

HETEROGENEOUS: different; diversified; mixed

HIATUS: interval; space; interruption

HICK: rustic; yokel; rube; hayseed; bumpkin

HIDDEN: unknown; obscure; secret; concealed; secluded; abstruse; latent

HIDEOUS: odious; ugly; repulsive; repugnant; offensive; revolting; disgusting; sickening; loathsome; vile; foul; nasty; obnoxious; detestable; nauseating; horrid; horrible; awful; dreadful; terrible

HIGH: great; lofty; excessive; expensive; proud; exalted

HIGHFALUTIN: bombast; grandiloquent; exaggerated; ostentatious; proud; boastful; arrogant

HILLARIOUS: merry; mirthful; joyful; joyous; gleeful; gleesome; jolly; jovial; jocular; festive

HINT: trace; tinge; clue; reminder; supposition; intimation

HIRE: rent; lease; commission; employ; engage; retain; enlist; charter

HIRELING: employee; mercenary; agent

HISS: deride; boo; sibilate

HISTORY: chronicle; record; annals; biography; tale; story; manual; book; volume

HISTRIONICS: dramatics; theatrics; affectation; pretentiousness

HOARD: store; collect; accumulate; amass; save; garner; heap; stockpile

HOARY: ancient; aged; frosty; gray

HOAX: canard; deception; deceit; spoof; humbug; flim-flam; fake; bogy; false-alarm

HOGGISH: porcine; greedy; filthy; gluttonous

HOLD: compartment; cellar; influence; control; custody; possession;

grasp; seizure; adhere; include; endure; transfix; maintain; decide; retain

HOLD BACK: delay; slow down; reserve; hinder; abstain; restrain; refuse; stint

HOLD FAST: adhere; be determined; persevere

HOLD FORTH: expound; speak; declaim; offer; propound

HOLD OFF: delay; temporize; repulse

HOLD ON: adhere; endure; wait; continue; retain; persevere

HOLD OUT: endure; stand fast; persevere; refuse; resist; offer

HOLDER: recipient; possessor; receptacle

HOLDUP: retardation; delay; robbery; overcharge

HOLE: hovel; lair; dive; nook; cellar; pit; cavity; cave; hiding place; filthy place

HOLLOW: pit; cavity; vacant; spacious; insincere

HOLY TERROR: hellion; frightener; violent person

HOMAGE: reverence; allegiance; worship

HOME: fatherland; country; nation; abode; habitat; asylum; infirmary; house; residence; dwelling; mansion; household

HOMELESS: alone; unplaced; destitute; forlorn; displaced

HOMESPUN: rough; coarse; vulgar; plain

HOMOGENEOUS: uniform; similar; simple

HONOR: repute; esteem; respect; praise; integrity

HONORABLE: reputable; upright; venerable

HOODLUM: ruffian; tough; roughneck; bruiser; rowdy; thug; hood; hooligan; desperado; cutthroat; muscleman; goon; gunman; torpedo; hatchetman

HOOK: fasten; tie; snare; catch; lure

HOPE: trust; expectation; desire; promise

HOPEFUL: probable; expectant; propitious

HOPELESS: futile; despondent; disconsolate; impossible

HORRID: terrible; odious; hideous; horrible

HORROR: distress; abhorrence; terror; disgust

HOST: throng; multitude; army; proprietor

HOSTILE: contrary; opposed; belligerent; unfriendly

HOSTILITY: contrariety; antisocialism; opposition; enmity

HOT: torrid; feverish; fervent; excited; anxious; angry; bothered; near; fugitive

HOT AIR: nonsense; bombast; brag; chatter

HOTHEADED: violent; excitable; impetuous

HOUSE: (see home) family; lineage; race; audience

HOVER: drift; float; soar; be imminent; be irresolute

HOWL: yell; plaint; objection; wail

HUBBUB: commotion; turbulence; uproar; outcry; bustle; agitation

HUCKSTER: advertiser; vendor; salesman; peddler

HUE AND CRY: outcry; alarm; publicity; search; chase

HUG: embrace; welcome; greeting; adhere; hold; seize; abut

HUMAN: mortal; merciful; kind
HUMBLE: conquer; subdue; humiliate; demean; inferior; contrite; lowly; modest
HUMILIATE: humble; affront; mortify; disgrace
HYPOTHESIS: premise; proposition; assumption; statement; supposition; inference; surmise; theory

I

IDEA: notion; opinion; meaning; understand
IDEAL: model; theoretical; typical perfect
IDENTIFICATION: recognition; sign; naming
IDIOSYNCRASY: characteristic; eccentricity; mannerism; temperament
IDIOTIC: foolish, crazy; feeble-minded
IDLE: loaf; inactive; leisure; trivial; vain
IFFY: provisory; doubtful; questionable
IGNOBLE: menial; plebeian; disreputable; vulgar
IGNORANT: unintelligent; unknowing; inexperienced; green
IGNORE: disregard; neglect; disobey; snub; condone
ILLEGAL: unlawful; illicit; lawless; wrongful; unauthorized; unconstitutional; criminal; felonious
ILLITERATE: unlearned; inerudite; uneducated; unschooled; untaught; unread; uncultured; lowbrow
ILL-REPUTE: disrepute; bad name; disesteem; dishonor; discredit; disfavor
ILLUMINATE: light up; color explain; adorn; picture
ILLUSORY: unfounded; unsubstantial; erroneous; delusory; imaginary; deceptive
ILLUSTRATE: demonstrate; exemplify; explain; represent; picture; cite
IMAGE: likeness; copy; telepicture; appearance; apparition; idea; illusion; symbol; representation; picture; photograph
IMAGINABLE: supposable; possible; fanciable
IMAGINE: suppose; fancy; think; judge
IMBIBE: take in; absorb; drink; learn
IMBUE: infuse; permeate; inculcate; affect
IMITATE: copy; ape; simulate
IMMACULATE: faultless; innocent; clean; chaste
IMMEDIATE: instantaneous; prompt; imminent; continuous; present; direct; nearest; adjoining
IMMENSE: great; infinite; superb; mammoth; vast; huge
IMMUNITY: exemption; exception; release; discharge; liberty
IMMUTABLE: obstinate; inflexible; unchangeable

IMPACT: collision; clash; encounter; bump; shock; brunt
IMPALE: pierce; stab; torture
IMPALPABLE: intangible; imponderable; infinitesimal; immaterial; unintelligible
IMPART: communicate; convey; give; inform; say; transfer
IMPARTIAL: unprejudiced; neutral; just
IMPASSIONED: vehement; zealous; passionate; excited; amorous
IMPATIENT: restive; eager; impetuous
IMPEDE: delay; retard; hinder; restrict; obstruct
IMPEL: drive; prompt; compel; propel; actuate; obsess
IMPENETRABLE: impregnable; impervious; inaccessible; unintelligible; dense
IMPERATIVE: urgent; necessary; mandatory; compulsory; obligatory
IMPERFECT: defective; impaired; blemished; immature; inferior; inadequate; slight
IMPERIOUS: urgent; compelling; obligatory; arrogant; masterful
IMPERSONATE: represent; enact; pose; act; masquerade
IMPETUOUS: sudden; hasty; impulsive; reckless; violent
IMPLICATE: involve; entangle; incriminate; imply; relate; enmesh; hint; suggest
IMPLICIT: inherent; implied; unqualified
IMPLY: involve; promise; mean; suggest; hint
IMPORTANT: influential; substantial; famous
IMPORTUNATE: necessary; urgent; insistent; compulsory; entreat
IMPOSE: intrude; deceive; exploit; presume on; inflect upon; levy
IMPOSING: grandiloquent; ceremonious; grandiose; dignified
IMPOSSIBLE: hopeless; inconceivable; unsatisfactory; terrible
IMPOTENT: incapable; powerless; weak; uninfluential; sterile
IMPRESS: mark; print; engrave; inculcate; fix in the mind; affect; conscript; commandeer; shanghai
IMPRESSION: copy; characteristic; effect; form; identation; sensation; appearance; idea; hunch; supposition; opinion
IMPRESSIVE: convincing; eloquent; dramatic; exciting; grandiose
IMPROPER: indecent; wrong; vulgar; naughty; inelegant; unsuitable; censure; deny; refute
IMPULSIVE: impelling; impetuous; hasty; instinctive; motivating
IMPUTATION: stigma; criticism; accusation; attribution; aspersion
IMPUTE: attribute; accuse; blame
IN COLD BLOOD: intentionally; unfeeling; cruelly
IN THE CARDS: imminent; possible; probable; liable; inevitable
IN ANY CASE: notwithstanding; provided; possibly; anyhow
INADEQUATE: unequal; deficient; insufficient; imperfect; inferior; incompetent; unsatisfactory
INAPPROPRIATE: irrelevant; inept; untimely; inexpedient
INATTENTIVE: heedless; negligent; distrusted
INCAPABLE: impotent; incompetent; unable; unqualified

INCENDIARY: arsonist; pyromaniac; firebug; instigator; inflamatory; incitive

INCESSANT: continuous; recurrent; constant; perpetual

INCIDENT: happening; event; occurrence; circumstance

INCITE: instigate; foment; agitate; excite; stir up; inflame; fire up; provoke; infuriate; irritate; madden; fan the flame; apply the torch

INCITER: instigator; provoker; agitator; fomenter; inflamer; rabble rouser; troublemaker

INCLINATION: tendency; leaning; direction; disposition; desire; intention

INCLINE: tend; lean; bear; gravitate

INCOMPETENT: impotent; incapable; unable; unqualified; unskillful

INCONCEIVABLE: fantastic; unbelievable; impossible; wonderful

INCONGRUOUS: differing; inconsistent; illogical; inappropriate

INCONSIDERATE: careless; unkind; incongruous; incoherent; fanatical; illogical

INCONSTANT: divergent; irregular; changeable; unfaithful; nonobserving

INCORPORATE: combine; include; embody; compose; affiliate

INCORRIGIBLE: wicked; bad; ungovernable

INCREASE: expand; grow; add; aggravate; multiply; intensify

INCREDIBLE: remarkable; fantastic; unbelievable; improbable; wonderful

INCRIMINATE: implicate; involve; attack; assail; inculpate

INDEFINITE: general; infinite; formless; indistinct; vague; neutral

INDEMNITY: compensation; security; recompense; amnesty; atonement

INDESCRIBABLE: extraordinary; inexpressible; inexplicable; wonderful

INDICATE: foretoken; mean; show; hint; signify; imply; evidence

INDICTMENT: arraignment; charge; presentment; information; accusation; complaint; blame

INDIFFERENCE: unconcern; apathy; neutrality; incuriosity

INDIFFERENT: insipid; unbiased; incurious; unconcerned; apathetic; neutral

INDIGENCE: penury; pauperism; impoverishment; destitution; privation; neediness; want; pennilessness

INDIGNANT: angry; angered; irate; mad; sore; worked-up

INDIGNITY: affront; offense; injury; insult; aspersion; outrage; atrocity

INDIRECT: devious; circuitous; deceitful; dishonest

INDISCRIMINATE: mixed; orderless; extensive; haphazard

INDISTINCT: dim; vague; obscure; faint

INDUCE: cause; persuade; infer; elicit

INDULGENCE: tolerance; leniency; permission; patience; considerate; forgiveness; intemperance

INEFFECTIVE: unable; ineffectual; uninfluential; unsuccessful
INELEGANT: clumsy; vulgar; indecent; unbeautiful
INEPT: inappropriate; unintelligent; unskillful; inexpedient
INEQUALITY: uneveness; disparity; odds; irregularity; disproportion; unbalance; imbalance; inadequacy; unequal; disparate
INEQUITY: injustice; unfairness; partiality; bias; favoritism; wrong; injury; grievance
INERT: motionless; listless; inanimate
INEXCUSABLE: unjustifiable; unpardonable; unforgivable; unallowable; indefensible
INEXPERIENCED: immature; ignorant; unpracticed
INEXTRICABLE: unsolvable; stuck; mired
INFAMOUS: wicked; disreputable; terrible; abominable
INFATUATE: enamor; charm; fascinate; captivate; bewitch; enrapture; obsess
INFATUATION: foolishness; craze; enthusiasm; love
INFECT: excite; inspire; corrupt; disease
INFER: deduce; suppose; imply; construe
INFERENCE: logic; deduction; supposition; implication
INFERIOR: subordinate; lower; poor; petty
INFERNAL: cruel; cursed; wicked; hellish
INFERRED: assumed; implied; stated
INFESTED: beset; ravaged; plagued; grubby
INFILTRATE: imbue; absorb; steep; filter-in
INFINITE: boundless; eternal; divine; omnipresent
INFIRM: aged; weak; feeble-minded; unsafe
INFLAME: ignite; incite; excite; anger; irritate; redden
INFLAMED: violent; hot; sore; feverish; excited
INFLATED: distended; bombastic; pompous; boastful
INFLEXIBLE: immovable; rigid; obstinate; strict
INFORM: tell; report; inspire; instruct
INFORMAL: unconventional; unmethodical; unceremonious; colloquial
INFORMATION: data; knowledge; enlightenment; news
INFRACTION: violation; breach; trespass; transgression; offense
INFREQUENT: sparse; occasional; spasmodic
INFRINGE: intrude; violate; overstep
INFURIATE: incite; irritate; enrage; antagonize
INFUSE: imbue; inculcate; inspire; baptize
INGENIOUS: skillful; resourceful; dextrous; deft; cunning
INGRAINED: intrinsic; established; habitual
INHABIT: occupy; reside; live; dwell; nest
INHALE: suck; breathe; smell; smoke
INHIBIT: hinder; restrain; prohibit
INHUMAN: savage; cruel; demonical
INIMICAL: contrary; opposed; unfriendly; belligerent
INITIATION: ceremony; inauguration; admission; preinstruction

INJURY: harm; impairment; loss; indignity; injustice
INMATE: inhabitant; occupant; tenant; resident; sojourner
INNOCENT: unsophisticate; childish; not guilty; harmless
INNOCUOUS: harmless; innocent; inoffensive
INNOVATION: novelty; change; introduction; new phase
INORDINATE: fanatical; excessive; exorbitant; intemperate
INQUIRE: ask; question; query; pursue; demand
INSANE: idiotic; lunatic; moronic; imbecile; nitwitted; foolish; mad
INSECURE: uncertain; unsafe; unreliable
INSENSIBLE: unaware; imperceptible; inanimate; inappreciable
INSIDIOUS: deceitful; dishonest; wily; cunning
INSIGNIFICANT: smallness; meaninglessness; unimportance
INSINUATION: hint; insertion; aspersion; interjection; intrusion
INSIPID: tasteless; prosaic; indifferent; mediocre; dull; wishy-washy
INSISTENT: persistent; demanding; urgent
INSOLENCE: defiance; arrogance; impudence; insult
INSPECTION: scrutiny; survey; review; perusal; study; contemplation
INSPIRATION: genius; intuition; motivation; encouragement; provocation
INSPIRE: cheer; encourage; prompt; provoke
INSTABILITY: weakness; unsafeness; irresolution; unreliability
INSTALL: admit; inaugurate; institute; instate; put in
INSTANTANEOUS: momentary; immediate; quick; prompt
INSTIGATION: incitement; stimulation; fomentation; agitation; provocation
INSTIGATOR: inciter; exciter; urger; provoker; provacator; agent; agitator; fomenter; inflamer; rabble rouser; ringleader; troublemaker
INSTRUCT: inform; teach; order; advise; direct
INSTRUMENT: tool; agent; medium; document
INSUFFICIENT: unequal; inadequate; unsatisfactory
INSULT: indignity; affront; offense; injury; aspersion; outrage; dishonor; humiliate; insolence; disrespect
INSURGENCE: revolt; rebellion; mutiny; insurrection; riot; uprising
INTACT: sound; whole; unchanged
INTEGRAL: whole; essential; component
INTELLIGENCE: intellect; understanding; sanity; knowledge; information; news
INTELLIGENT: sensible; sane; knowing
INTEMPERATE: excessive; unrestrained; inabstinent; gluttonous
INTENSE: great; violent; vivid; energetic
INTENT: intention; purpose; aim; object; design; plan; attentive; zealous
INTENTION: meaning; motive; purpose; determination
INTERCEDE: mediate; intervene; negotiate; arbitrate; referee
INTEREST: relevance; concern; cause; influence; curiosity; motive; incentive; involver; excite; attract

126

INTERFERE: intrude; hinder; intervene

INTERLUDE: interim; pause; respite

INTERMEDIARY: medium; go-between; mediator; middle; intervening

INTERMINABLE: continuous; infinite; perpetual; long

INTERPOSE: interject; intrude; mediate; come between

INTERPRETATION: meaning; explanation; diagnosis

INTERROGATION: questioning; querying; inquiring; quiz; examination; challenge; dispute

INTERRUPT: stop; intrude; hinder

INTERRUPTION: intermission; interim; pause; interval; intrusion; hindrance

INTERVAL: degree; interruption; period; interim; pause

(AT) INTERVALS: haphazardly; intermittently; occasionally; irregularly

INTERVENE: intrude; mediate; come between; interpose

INTIMATE: friend; ally; hint; announce; near; sociable; friendly

INTIMATED: implied; meant; suggested; insinuated; hinted; inferred; supposed; assumed; presumed

INTIMATION: trace; hunch; supposition; omen; hint; clue

INTIMIDATE: threaten; menace; cow; browbeat; bulldoze; bully; harass; terrorize

INTOLERANT: bigot; illiberal; fanatic; unsympathetic; uncharitable; unindulgent; ungenerous; deaf

INTRANSIGENT: conservative; obstinate; uncompromising

INTREPID: courageous; brave; bold; valiant; gallant; heroic

INTRICATE: complex; complicated; confused; involved; elaborate; knotty

INTRIGUE: plot; scheme; artifice; fascinate; delight; allure

INTRODUCE: inaugurate; originate; innovate; acquaint; submit; insert

INUNDATE: flood; submerge; overflow; oversupply

INURE: callous; harden; accustom

INVADE: intrude; infest; attack

INVALIDATE: disqualify; disprove; annul; neutralize; disable

INVARIABLY: uniformly; universally; always

INVASION: intrusion; attack; infestation

INVEIGLE: lure; entice; seduce; ensnare; entrap; enmesh; involve

INVEST: empower; clothe; wrap; instate; endow; provide; risk; venture

INVESTIGATE: explore; probe; sound; fathom; look into; delve

INVESTIGATION: discussion; debate; deliberation; review; examination; exploration; probing; delving into

INVETERATE: traditional; established; habitual

INVIGORATE: strengthen; energize; refresh; stimulate; cheer

INVITE: ask; interest; encourage; tempt; provoke

INVOKE: appeal; address; entreat; pray; conjure
INVOLUNTARY: unintentional; instinctive; unwilling; unwitting
INVOLVE: concern; complicate; entail; implicate; envelop; interest; absorb; imply; ensnare; incriminate
INVULNERABLE: impregnable; unassailable; invincible; unbeatable
IRATE: angry; angered; indignant; wrathful; mad; worked up
IRK: annoy; anger; tire; weary; vex
IRREGULAR: abnormal; inconsistent; distorted; rough; informal; haphazard
IRRESOLUTE: uncertain; undecided; capricious; fickle
IRRESPONSIBLE: untrustworthy; fickle; lawless
IRREVOCABLE: past; unchangeable; inevitable; mandatory
IRRITATE: incite; excite; annoy; anger; provoke
ISOLATED: unrelated; separated; alone; secluded
ISSUE: cause; effect; product; posterity; emergence; topic; question; solution; publication; edition; disperse; ensue; result; emerge; flow; distribute; print
ITEM: circumstance; part; piece; memorandum; commodity
ITERATION: recapitulation; retelling; recounting; restatement; rehash; elaboration

J

JAB: blow; knock; tap; rap; slap; hit; swipe; thrust; lunge
JABBER: stammer; chatter; unmeaning
JAIL: prison; cage; coop; cell; penitentiary; clink; can; stir; pen; reformatory; imprison; arrest
JAR: vessel; clash; agitation; discord
JAUNDICED: yellow; prejudiced; dejected; jealous; disapproval
JEALOUSY: envy; lust; covet; crave; jaundiced; suspicion
JERK: pull; start; throw; agitate
JILT: disappoint; deceive; dishonor
JOG: advance; shake; push; trudge
JOIN: connect; assemble; marry; enlist; discuss; contend
JOKE: absurdity; trifle; ridicule; wit; jest; farce
JOLLY: gay; plump; ridicule
JOURNAL: annals, newspaper; record; magazine; narrative; account; log
JOURNALIST: recorder; author; writer; essayist; publicist; scribe; penman; correspondent; scribbler; reporter
JOURNEY: excursion; expedition; tour; trip; pilgrimage; trek; march; walk; hike; promenade; outing
JOVIAL: gay; amusing; social
JOY: pleasure; gratification; enjoyment; relish; zest; delight; glee; cheer; happiness

JUBILANT: gay; rejoicing; boastful

JUDGE: jurist; umpire; referee; arbiter; assessor; critic; conclude; ascertain; determine; deduce; estimate; value; assess; rate; consider; think; settle; decide; try; rule; award; comment; criticize; review; investigate

JUDGMENT: intellect; discrimination; decision; wisdom; sentence

JUDICIOUS: wise; sage; sagacious; reasonable; rational; sound; sensible; impartial; equitable; fair; thoughtful

JUMBLE: mixture; confusion; indiscrimination; derange

JUST: accurate; right; equitable; pious; similar; exact

JUSTICE: right; equity; impartiality; fair play; square deal

JUVENILE: young; youthful; green; budding; under age

K

KEEL: even; tilt; careen

KEEL OVER: overturn; capsize; faint

KEEN: energetic; acrimonious; violent; sharp; pungent; shrill; smart; alert; eager; good; fervent; caustic

KEEP: maintain; preserve; retain; sustain; reserve; observe; obey

KEEP BACK: delay; retard; reserve; hinder; restrain

KEEP DOWN: oppress; supress; subjugate

KEEP FROM: avoid; refrain; prevent; restrain; abstain

KEEP OFF: repulse; prevent; ward off

KEEP ON: continue; persevere; endure

KEEP UP: continue; support; persevere

KEEPING: conformity; symmetry; protection; custody; observance; retention

KEN: see; perception; knowledge; know; understand

KEY: opener; tone; clue; fundamental

KEYSTONE: important thing; arch; cornerstone

KICK: foot; blow; recoil; protest; complaint; strike; object; complain

KICKBACK: repayment; reimbursement; return; restitution; refund

KID: goat; hoax; fool; banter; sport; twit; jest; joke; josh; nag; tease; rib; razz; ridicule

KIDNAP: abduct; abduce; shanghai; impress; snatch

KILL: excise; slay; silence; destroy; defeat; suppress; veto; execute; pain; torture

KILLING: slaying; execution; success; deadly; alluring; exhausting; exciting; delightful; amusing; humorous; beautiful

KIN: relatives; relations; people; kinsmen; kinsfolk

KIND: indulgent; complaint; complaisant; obliging; accommodating; agreeable; amiable; gracious; generous; decent; lenient; benign; good; nice; warmhearted; softhearted; tender; sympathetic; human; humane

KINDLE: ignite; incite; excite

KINK: complication; crinkle; crack; caprice; expedient
KNACK: talent; skill; adeptness; expertise; proficiency; adroitness; skillfulness
KNEAD: mix; form; massage; stroke
(on bended) KNEE: submissive; supplicatory; humbled; obsequious; obeisant; worshipful
KNEEL: truckle; submit; entreat; make obeisant
KNIT: fasten; contract; wrinkle; interlace; heal
KNOB: hill; head; protruberance; sphere
KNOCK: blow; bang; criticism; collide; strike; criticize; disparage; pound
KNOCK (down): fell; raze; unnerve; deject; auction off
KNOCK (off): deduct; stop; die; write; improvise; accomplish
KNOCKOUT: quietus; stopper; finisher; clincher; flattener; kayo; cincher; capper; coup de grace
KNOT: complication; tie; distortion; bulge; problem; dilemna; tangle; distort; knit; lump
KNOTTY: rough; difficult; abstruse
KNOW: sense; experience; recognize; be certain; intuition; informed; skilled
KNOWLEDGEABLE: knowing; cognizant; conscious; aware; mindful; sensible; intelligent; understanding; comprehending; hep; perceptive; shrewd; sagacious; wise; omniscient
KOSHER: clean; pure; clear; immaculate; taintless; unsoiled; untarnished; undefiled
KOWTOW: truckle; be submissive; make obeisance
KUDOS: fame; renown; glory; recognition; repute

L

LABEL: adjunct; tab; symbol; earmark; sign; marker; emblem; badge
LABOR: work; exertion; punishment
LABOR (UNDER): difficulty; affliction; feeling
LABYRINTH: disorder; secret; convolution
LACE: stitch; join; connect; unite; tack; knit; entwine; netting
LACERATE: cut; incise; disjoin; disconnect; detach; separate; sunder; divide; severe; slit; slice
LACERATION: disassociation; separation; parting; detachment; break; rupture; dismemberment; severance; fissure; breach; split; incision; slit; dissection
LACK: need; require; want; insufficiency; inadequacy; deficiency; shortcoming; scarcity
LACKADAISICAL: inactive; melancholy; indifferent
LAD: boy; youth; stripling; youngster; minor
LADY: woman; female; madam; Mrs.; matron; dowager

LAG: linger; dwadle; follow

LAIR: den; cave; hole; hiding place; diggings

LAME: impotent; weak; imperfect; diseased; injure

LAMENT: mourn; deplore; grieve; bemoan; sorrow; sadness; cry; weep; sob; blubber; whimper; groan; moan

LAMENTABLE: sad; painful; bad

LAMENTATION: complaint; wail; murmur; grumble; moan; whimper; sob; cry; weep; mourning; knell

LAND: arrive; debark; disembark; alight; deplane; detrain; dismount; anchor; earth; ground; terra firma; soil; real estate; acreage; estate; property; plot; site; territory; parcel

LANE: opening; aperture; pathway; channel; aisle; path; route; course; artery; corridor

LANGUID: weak; inactive; inert; slow; torpid

LARGE: sizable; bulky; huge; enormous; immense; monstrous; gargantuan; mammoth; big; great; considerable; voluminous; massive; spacious; mighty; corpulent; fat; stout; vast; stupendous

LARK: fun; frolic; merriment; pleasantry; prank; antic; spree; diversion

LASH: tie; punish; scourge; censure; incite

LAST: continue; endure; remain; stay; persist; survive

LATENT: dormant; smolder; unexerted; hidden; concealed; lurk; underlie; commote; allude; infer; imply; secret; below the surface; behind the scene

LATITUDE: freedom; scope; range; extent

LAUD: admire; command; praise; eulogize; applaud; approve; esteem; prize; sanction; endorse; compliment; acclaim; extol

LAUGH: giggle; titter; chuckle; snicker; guffaw; rejoice; exult

LAUGH (AT): ridicule; deride; snigger; scoff; mock; banter; roast; sarcastic; sneer

LAVISH: excessive; profuse; voluminous; give; bestow; present; waste; dissipate

LAZY: inactive; indolent; dwadling; dull; languorous; drowsy; idle; slack; leaden

LEAD: pioneer; influence; tend; induce; direct; authority; important; star

LEADEN: dim; gray; colorless; inactive

LEADER: counselor; director; precursor

LEAK: crack; injury; disclosure; waste; dribble

LEANING: tendency; favoritism; willingness; desire

LEARN: know; conceive; comprehend; understand; discern; perceive

LEAVE: relinquish; permission; bequeath; depart; freedom; disappear

LECTURE: teach; speak; censure; sermon; dissertation

LEDGE: projection; shelf

LEER: look; glimpse; peep; gaze; stare; ogle

LEFT: residue; remainder; remains; balance; surviving; nearside; portside

LEGAL: lawful; licit; legitimate; allowable; permitted; sanctioned; authorized

LEGEND: description; narrative; history; memoir; annals, saga; epic; story; tale; journal

LEGENDARY: fabulous; mythological; imaginary; fanciful; fantastic; fairy-like

LEGION: host; many; great; numerous; manifold; array; phalanx

LEGITIMATE: true; right; due; legal; permitted

LEND: loan; advance; accommodate; intrust; aid; help; assist

LENIENT: moderate; mild; compassionate

LESS: inferior; minor; deficient; smaller; minus; lower; under; subtraction; deduction

LETHAL: mortal; fatal; deadly; suicidal

LETHARGY: sleepy; drowsy; torpidity; dreamy

LEVEL: uniform; equal; flat; horizontal; smooth; destroy

LEVITY: lightness; irresolution; trifle; rashness; jocularity

LIABILITY: possibility; contingency; incurable; accountability; debt; obligation; duty; onus; responsibility; obligation

LIAR: deceiver; hypocrite; sophist; fraud; cheat; swindler; prevaricator

LIBEL: detraction; disparagement; vilification; scurrility; scandal; defamation; aspersion; traducement; slander; calumny

LICENSE: permission; right; exemption; laxity

LIGHT: match; kindle; luminosity; levity; gay; easy; small; wee; arrive; descend; aspect; knowledge; interpretation; unimportant; luminary; facilitate

(BRING TO) LIGHT: disclose; discover; manifest

(MAKE) LIGHT (OF): underrate; despise; easy; inexcitable

LIGHT (UP): illuminate; cheer; excite

LIGHT (UPON): acquire; discover; chance; arrive at

LIKE: relish; enjoy; love; similar; wish; hope

LIMIT: complete; end; circumscribe; restrain; prohibit

LIMP: supple; weak; slow; fail

LINEAGE: ancestry; posterity; kindred; series

LINGER: loiter; delay; protract

LINK: connection; relation; part; portion

LIST: catalog; record; docket; account; roster; enroll; schedule; register; post; tally; index; enumerate

LISTLESS: inattentive; inactive; indifferent

LITIGATION: quarrel; contention; lawsuit

LIVELY: keen; active; sprightly; acute

LOAD: quantity; cargo; weight; fill; lode; store; hindrance; oppress; anxiety; adversity

LOATHSOME: dislike; painful; unsavory

LOCK: fasten; fastening; imprison; hindrance; restrain

LOOK: appearance; view; attention; care; seek; expect; intention; examine

LOOPHOLE: opening; device; escape

LOOSE: detach; liberate; free; permit; incoherent; illogical; vague; lag; desultory; indulgent

LOSE: forget; fail; regress; neglect; wander

LOST: absent; invisible; abstracted; uncertain; dejected

LOT: quantity; group; horde; multitude

LOVE: affection; desire; want; courtesy; favorite

LOW: base; vulgar; common; disreputable; small; inferior; depressed; mutter; moo

LOWER: inferior; decrease; depress; dim; sad; dark; irate; sulky

LUCID: luminous; intelligible; transparent

LUKEWARM: temperate; indifferent; torpid; irresolute

LULL: cessation; silence; mitigate

LUMP: whole; chief part; mass; weight; density; amass

LURE: attract; entice; deceive

LUXURIOUS: pleasant; delightful; intemperate

M

MACHINATION: trick; plan; cunning

MACHINE: instrument; mechanism; contrivance; implement; utensil

MAD: insane; deranged; unsound; excited; feverish; fuming; raving; raging; frantic; distraught

MAELSTROM: pitfall; eddy; whirlpool

MAGAZINE: periodical; journal; book

MAGNETISM: attraction; influence; power; motive

MAGNIFICENT: fine; grand; large

MAGNIFY: increase; enlarge; exaggerate; overrate

MAID: servant; girl; lass; spinster

MAIN: principal; prominent; material; notable; salient; critical; paramount; essential; vital; prime; primary; foremost

(IN THE) MAIN: principally; greatly; intrinsically; on the whole

MAIN (FORCE): compulsion; violence; strength

MAINSTAY: hope; refuge; support

MAINTAIN: permanence; continue; sustain; preserve; support; assert

MAJOR: greater; higher; distinguishing; superior; foremost; crowing; supreme

MAKE: form; produce; constitute; render; complete; compel

MAKE (GOOD): complete; provide; restore; compensate; demonstrate; establish

MALADY: sickness; disease; illness; infection; afflicted; unsound; tainted

MALCONTENT: opponent; antagonist; adversary; rival; enemy; assailant; brawler; disputant; reactionist; demagogue; dissident; hypocritical; dissatisfied

MALE: man; gentleman; sir; fellow; guy; chap; mister

MALEFACTION: misconduct; misbehavior; malpractice; transgression; sin; dereliction; indiscretion; peccadillo; crime; felony

MALEFACTOR: badman; wrongdoer; sinner; rascal; scoundrel; villain; miscreant; reprobate; delinquent; criminal

MALIGN: detract; disparage; deprecate; vilify; defame; slander; libel; derogate; traduce

MALTREAT: injure; molest; aggrieve

MAN: servant; adult; male

MANAGE: direct; govern; conduct; prescribe; superintend; supervise; control; administer; succeed; triumph; surmount; overcome; prosper

MANDAMUS: command; order; fiat; decree; enjoin; instruct

MANDATE: order; injunction; ultimatum; command; charge

MANIA: insanity; madness; frenzy; fanaticism; craze; eccentricity; desire; wish; fancy; need; passion; rage

MANIAC: madman; lunatic; raver; eccentric; nut; fanatic; idiot; madcap

MANIFEST: disclose; obvious; visible; list

MANIFESTO: announcement; publication; proclamation; pronouncement

MANIPULATE: handle; use; conduct

MANLY: adolescent; male; strong; brave; honest

MANNER: style; way; conduct

MANNERISM: affectation; unconformity; vanity

MANEUVER: action; performance; exercise; movement; operation; execution; procedure; act; measure

MANY: multitude; numerous; multiplicity; repeated; frequent; profusion; host; legion; great; large; array; galaxy; swarm; flock; lots; loads; heaps

MAR: injure; damage; despoil; blacken; spoil; cripple

MARCH: journey; trip; walk; step; trend; pace; plod; stride; wend; trudge; tramp; stride; progress; advance; proceed

(STEAL A) MARCH: advance; deceive; cunning; active

MARGIN: space; latitude; edge; rim

MARK: degree; repute; importance; term; indicate; object; record; writing; take cognizance of; affirm

MARROW: essence; central; interior

MASH: pulpify; mix; soft; semiliquid; disorder

MASK: shade; shield; conceal; ambush; deceive; disguise

MASS: quantity; much; heap; whole; size; worship; rite

MASSACRE: destruction; killing; murder; assassination; slaughter; carnage; butchery; pogrom

MASSIVE: large; huge; heavy; dense

MASTER: boy; man; know; understand; proficient; learn; succeed; conquer; teacher; director; possessor

MATCH: marriage; contest; similar; copy; equal; coincide

MATCHLESS: supreme; excellent; virtuous

MATERIAL: substance; object; bodily; physical; tangible; substantial; matter; stuff; element; principle

MATTER: material; substance; topic; meaning; type

MATTER (OF COURSE): conformity; habitual; certain

MATURE: aged; old; adolescent; complete; perfect; improve; prepare

MAXIMUM: supreme; major; greatest; predominent

MAZE: difficulty; enigma; disorder; convolution

MEAGER: small; thin; poor; scanty; incomplete

MEAN: average; middle; small; intend; signify; base; selfish; contemptible; stingy; shabby; ignoble; sneaking; express; connote; convey; imply; allude

MEANING: significance; sense; expression; purport; drift; tenor; implication; connotation; essence; scope; spirit

MEANWHILE: during; pending; meantime; interim; throughout; all along

MEASURE: extent; degree; apportion; calculate; compute; proceeding

MEASURED: temperate; moderate; sufficient

MEDIATION: intervention; interference; intercession; parley; negotiation; arbitration; diplomacy; compromise

MEDIOCRITY: average; smallness; imperfect

MEDITATE: think; reflect; cogitate; consider; deliberate; speculate; contemplate; ponder; muse; dream; ruminate; study

MEDIUM: mean; middle; oracle; seer; imposter; instrument

MEET: assemble; converge; arrive; fulfill; agreement; touch

MEET (HALF WAY): willing; concord; pacification; mediation; compromise

MELANCHOLY: sadness; dejection; blues; dumps; despondency; disconsolate; depression; heavy-heart

MELLOW: old; soft; improve; tipsy

MELT: convert; liquefy; fuse

MELT (AWAY): disappear; decrease; cease to exist; waste

MEMBER: part; component; constituent; personnel

MEMENTO: sourvenir; token; keepsake; remembrance; suggestion

MEMORY: remembrance; recognition; retrospection; reminding; retention; impression; thoughts; recollection

MEND: improve; restore; draw; reconstruct; renovate; repair; renew; heal

MENTION: acquaint; instruct; communicate

MENTOR: teacher; advisor; sage

MERCENARY: parsimonious; selfish; price; soldier; servant

MERCHANDISE: commodities; wares; effects; goods; articles; stock; produce; cargo; market; sell

MERCY: leniency; tolerance; gentleness; indulgence; clemency; pity; compassion; tenderness

MERE: simple; small; trifle

MERGE: combine; insert; include; become
MERIT: goodness; virtue; due; right; entitle; deserve
MERRY: cheerful; gay; genial; hilarious; laughing
MESS: mixture; disorder; difficulty; failure; unskilled; meal
MESSAGE: news; information; report; story; intelligence; tidings; dispatch; communication; instruction
METE: dole; distribute; give; measure
METHOD: order; course; way; routine; manner; form; mode; fashion
METTLE: excite; encourage; brave; spirit; resolve; energy; sensitivity
MIGHT: power; energy; violence; may; maybe
MIGHTY: much; large; strong; haughty
MILD: moderate; lenient; courteous; calm; warm insipid
MILITANT: contending; contentious; bristling; belligerent; bellicose; martial
MILLENNIUM: utopia; hope; future
MIMIC: imitate; copy; repeat; duplicate; mock; impersonate
MIND: will; willing; desire; intellect; remember; believe; dislike; warning; purpose; care; attend; think
MINIMIZE: decrease; lessen; diminution; reduce; shrink; abridge; lower; belittle; underrate; underestimate; detract; derogate
MINISTER: give; aid; remedy; clergyman; director; ambassador; deputy
MINOR: inferior; small; less; lower; secondary; subaltern; infant; child; youth; youngster; stripling
MINUS: less; subtracted; absent; deficient; loss
MIRACLE: phenomenon; wonder; marvel; freak; portent; sign
MISCELLANY: compendium; collection; mixture; generality
MISCHIEF: evil; harm; hurt; nuisance; injury; badness; wrong; aggrieve; maltreat
MISDEED: misconduct; misbehavior; malpractice; transgression; offense; trespass; misdemeanor; crime
MISERABLE: unhappy; contemptible; small; dissatisfied; displeased; uneasy; vexed; discontent; annoyed; irritated; distressed; concerned; gloomy; heartbroken; wretched; desolate; pained; worried
MISFORTUNE: adversity; bad luck; trouble; hardship; curse; blight; disaster; calamity; catastrophe; accident; setback
MISTAKE: error; failure; misconstrue; mismanage
MITIGATE: relieve; improve; abate; extenuate
MOCK: initate; repeat; ridicule; disrespect; chuckle; deceive
MODE: habit; method; fashion; state
MODEL: copy; prototype; form; sculpture; representation; rule; perfection; good (man-boy-girl)
MODERATE: small; average; cheap; sufficient; slow; temperate; allay
MODERATOR: mediator; judge; director
MOLD: condition; convert; form; structure; curve; model; decay; vegetation; earth

MOLEST: pain; annoy; irritate; offend; hurt; tease; irk; vex; torture; torment; provoke; aggrieve; maltreat

MONOTONOUS: dull; weary; uniform; equal; repetition

MONSTROUS: excessive; exceptional; huge; ugly; vulgar; ridiculous; wonderful

MOOD: nature; state; tendency; temper; willingness

MORAL: right; virtuous; maxim; judgment; right

MORTIFICATION: pain; vexation; discontent; humiliation

MOTION: moving; topic; plan; proposal; request

MOTTO: maxim; phrase; device

MOUNT: increase; ascend; raise; display; hill; horse

MOUTH: entrance; opening; estuary; brink; eat; state; enunciate; speak

MOVE: motion; begin; propose; undertake; act; induce; offer; excite

MUDDLE: disorder; derange; absurd; failure; difficulty; inattention

MUDDY: moist; dim; opaque; stupid

MUFFLE: wrap; silent; deaden; conceal

MURKY: dark; opaque; gloomy; black

MUTE: speechless; silent; taciturn; sordine

MUTILATE: injure; deform; retrench

MUTTER: mumble; grumble; threaten

MUZZLE: silence; restrain; gag; make powerless

MYSTERIOUS: invisible; uncertain; obscure; concealed; latent; secret; puzzling

MYSTIFY: deceive; hide; falsify

MYTH: imagination; fancy; invention; figment; dream; vision; fantasy; whim; fib; lie; falsehood; fiction; fable; farce

N

NAB: arrest; capture; apprehend; seize; pinch

NABOB: personage; governor; rich man

NAG: pester; henpeck; pick on; carp at; fuss at; pick at; shrew; horse; colt; filly; stallion; pony; scalawag; goat

NAIL: fix; fasten; attach; affix; secure; tighten; nab; collar; capture

NAIVE: unsophisticate; innocent; a square; gullible; exploitable; artless; simple; unsuspicious

NAKED: nude; unadorned; exposed; unprotected; open

NAME: appellation; designation; cognomen; title; label; tag; personage; notable; dignitary; V.I.P; star; celebrity; luminary; reputation; fame; renown; specify; cite; nominate; appoint; call; denominate

NAP: doze; drowse; snooze; siesta; forty winks; slumber; texture; pile; shag, roughness; smoothness

NAPPING: unaware; bemused; inattentive

NARCOTIC: addict; fiend; dope fiend; opiate; drug; dope; opium; snow

NARRATE: tell; relate; recount; report; recite

NARRATIVE: narration; recital; review; story; yarn; account

NARROW: inlet; strait; contruct; taper; limit; qualify; slender

NARROW (MINDED): small; mean; petty; bigoted; strait-laced; meager; poor; meticulous

NARROW (ESCAPE): close call; close shave; squeak; tight squeeze

NASTINESS: obscenity; repugnance; filthiness; odiousness; unsavoriness

NASTY: unsavory; foul; odious; obscene

NATIONALITY: race; nation; statehood; nativity; community

NATIVE: primitive; aborigine; old timer; citizen; inhabitant; settler; inate; indigenous; natural; genuine

NATURAL: inate; lifelike; normal; genuine; typical; raw; artless; unaffected

NATURALLY: normally; genuinely; plainly; informally

NATURE: essence; kind; characteristic; tendency

NAUSEATE: offend; sicken; disgust; appall; horrify

NEAR: resemble; imminent; approach; related; approximate; imitation; close; intimate; about; at

NEARLY: about; almost; narrowly

NEARNESS: relation; likeness; closeness; intimacy

NEARSIGHTED: narrow-minded; undiscerning; myopic; unperceptive

NEAT: tidy; trim; clean; spruced; straight; groomed; elegant

NEBULOUS: dim; cloudy; obscure

NECESSARY: requirement; need; want; prerequisite; essential; compulsory; obligatory; urgent; imperative

NECESSITY: compulsion; obligation; urgency; requirement; need; want; prerequisite; essential; neediness; lack

NEED: deficiency; requirement; lack; poverty

NEEDLE: sew; pierce; goad; tease

NEFARIOUS: terrible; infamous; wicked

NEGATE: disprove; deny; refuse

NEGLECT: inattention; negligence; slight; snub; unconcern; procrastinate; slovenliness

NEGOTIATE: hurdle; pass; manage; mediate; bargain

NEIGHBORHOOD: region; environs; area; proximity

NEITHER HERE NOR THERE: irrelevant; nowhere; unimportant

NEITHER HOT NOR COLD: irresolute; indifferent; neutral; mediocre

NEITHER ONE THING NOR THE OTHER: insipid; indifferent; neutral; mediocre

NEOPHYTE: novice; beginner; freshman; tenderfoot; newcomer; rooky

NERVE: courage; spunk; pluck; grit; backbone; guts; insolence; gall; cheek; crust

NERVOUS: jittery; excitable; agitated

NERVY: strong; bold; impudent

NEST: lodging; abode; haunt; breeding place; multitude; settle; reside

NESTLE: cuddle; snuggle; protect

NET: profit; gain; snare; catch; crisscross; weave

NETTLE: incite; annoy; anger; provoke

NEUTRAL: nonpartisan; independent; unbiased; indifferent

NEUTRALIZE: offset; nullify; cushion; counteract

NEVER: always; invariably; universally

NEVERENDING: continuous; perpetual; always

NEW: additional; extra; fresh; unused; original; virgin; untried; novel; modern; recent

NEWS: tidings; intelligence; information; advice; article; story; message; dispatch; communication; communique; letter; telegram; bulletin; report

NEWS ANALYST: commentator; expounder; annotator; publicist

NEWSCASTER: reporter; broadcaster; commentator; announcer; spieler; radiocaster; telecaster

NEXT: subsequently; later; after; afterwards; thereafter; succeeding; nearest

NICE: savory; tasteful; detailed; precise; meticulous; fastidious; scrupulous; discriminative; suitable; good; pleasant; kind; proper

NIGHTMARE: hallucination; dream; horror; ogre

NIHILIST: destroyer; anarchist; radical

NIMBLE: fast; alert; quick; agile; smart

NIP: drink; small amount; dram; pinch; bite; cold; pang; pungency; hold; cut off; sever; shorten; chill; freeze; grip; catch; steal

NIP IN THE BUD: prevent; destroy; kill

NO: negative; con; nay; negation; denial; nope; nix; certainly not

NOBILITY: greatness; magnificence; aristocracy; dignity; distinction; eloquence

NOBLE: great; important; excellent; grandiose; dignified; reputable; honorable; magnanimous

NOD: assent; signal; bid; greet; obseisance; go to sleep; bow

NOISE: static; sound; racket; discord; din

NOISY: loud; vociferous; blustering

NOMINAL: so called; inexpensive; substantive; topical

NONESSENTIAL: extrinsic; incidental; irrelevant; superfluous; needless

NONPLUS: quandary; impasse; baffle; thwart

NONSENSE: absurdity; ridiculousness; ludicrousness; preposterousness; absurd; ridiculous; ludicrous; preposterous; outrageous; meaninglessness; poppycock; rubbish; humbug; folderol; buncombe; balderdash; piffle; fiddlesticks; applesauce; baloney

NOOSE: circle; snare, loop; catch; hangman's rope

NORMAL: average; natural; orderly; typical; same

NOSE: prow; snout; nozzle; meddle; push; nuzzle; smell; trace; pry; discover

NOSE (OUT): excel; defeat; thwart; humiliate; disappoint

NOSTALGIA: wistfulness; homesickness; sentimentality

NOTABILITY: greatness; obviousness; important; personage; repute; celebrity

NOTABLE: personage; celebrity; remarkable; obvious; important; famous

NOTE: observation; attention; comment; memorandum; memo; certificate; remark; epistle; reputation; heed; indicate; record

NOTEWORTHY: remarkable; special; notable; extraordinary

NOTHING: nonexistence; void; trifle

(HAVE) NOTHING (TO DO WITH): ignore; reject; avoid; refuse; abstain

NOTICE: observation; critique; attention; information; announcement; commentary; warning; order; inform; announce; warn; see; detect; heed; care

NOTICEABLE: remarkable; appreciable; visible; obvious

NOTIFICATION: information; announcement; warning; order; reminder

NOTIFY: remind; inform; announce; warn

NOTION: idea; supposition; opinion; caprice; impulse; intention

NOURISH: feed; nutrify; encourage; nurture

NOVEL: book; opus; story; fictional form; short story; original; fresh; unique; authentic; new; different; strange; unusual; uncommon; unfamiliar

NOW: at once; henceforth; instantly; the present; today; without delay; instantaneous

NUB: salient point; essential; fundamental; gist; crux

NUCLEUS: gist; center; rudiment

NUDE: unadorned; naked; undecorated; unfurbished; untrimmed; undressed; bare; bald; unclad; unclothed; undraped; raw; in the altogether

NULLIFY: neutralize; repeal; annihilate

NUMBER: quantity; kind; numeral; sum; amount; limit

NURSE: suckle; nurture; cherish; care for

NURTURE: feed; train; encourage; foster; cherish

NUT: fastener; head; lunatic; fanatic; eccentric; enthusiast

O

OAF: dolt; clumsy; fellow; changeling

OATH: deposition; pledge; curse

OBDURATE: insensible; obstinate; strict; heartless; hardened

OBEDIENCE: conformity; submission; compliance; authority

OBEISANT: submissive; reverential; pays homage

OBESE (ITY): corpulence; stoutness; fat; beefiness; gross; fleshy; beefy; plump; rotund; pudgy; thickset; chubby; stocky; burly; portly

OBEY: submit; comply; acquiesce; accede; mind; heed; observe; keep; regard; yield

OBJECT: article; thing; gadget; purpose; aim; end; goal; destination; target; meaning; intention; design; protest; kick; squawk; remonstrate; expostulate; dispute; challenge; demur; disapprove

OBJECTION: demurrer; protest; obstacle

OBJECTIVE: thing; purpose; extroverted; extrinsic

OBLIGATE: oblige; require; bind; pledge; beholden; indebted

OBLIGATION: condition; necessity; compulsion; promise; debt; kindness; duty

OBLIGATORY: necessary; mandatory; compulsory; incumbent upon

OBLIGE: compel; indulge; favor; accommodate; obligate

OBLITERATE: erase; efface; blot out; cancel; delete; expunge; raze; wipeout

OBLIVION: unconsciousness; stupor; forgetfulness; unfeeling

OBLIVIOUS: unconscious; heedless; abstracted; forgetful; unfeeling; asleep

OBNOXIOUS: nasty; terrible; infamous; odious; unsavory; disreputable

OBSCENE: lewd; bawdy; ribald; pornographic; salacious; lurid; dirty; smutty; impure; foul; filthy; nasty; vile; offensive; scurrilous

OBSCURE: dark; black; darken; blacken; opaque; cloud; blind; conceal; formless; dim; indistinct; vague; unrenouned

OBSERVANCE: conformity; watching; attention; vigilance; custom; ceremony; behavior; keeping; celebration; rite

OBSERVATION: watching; idea; opinion; attention; keeping remark

OBSERVE: conform; see; examine; heed; remark; obey; keep; celebrate

OBSESS: possess; haunt; bewitch; demonize; infatuate

OBSESSION: mania; craze; infatuation; enthusiasm; passion; fascination; fancy; bug

OBSOLETE: passe; extinct; dead; past; outworn

OBSTACLE: obstruction; block; blockade; bar; barrier; impediment; congestion; bottleneck; hindrance; difficulty; hurdle; deterrent; objection; stumbling block; snag

OBSTINATE: opinionated; dogmatic; positive; arbitrary; pragmatic; doctrinary; stubborn; willful; headstrong; pigheaded

OBSTREPEROUS: turbulent; blatant; vociferous; disobedient; ungovernable

OBSTRUCT: delay; clog; retard; hinder

OBTAIN: get; exist; prevail; induce; fetch; acquire; receive

OBSTRUSIVE: intrusive; hindering; garish; presumptuous

OBTUSE: blunt; insensitive; stupid; unfeeling

OBVIOUS: distinct; plain; clear; evident; patent; definite; defined;

clearcut; conspicuous; prominent; manifest; apparent; explicit; visible; noticeable

OCCASION: event; incident; circumstance; cause; motive; opportunity

OCCASIONAL: incidental; infrequent; casual; contingent

OCCUPATION: business; engrossment; habitation; possession; employment

OCCUPY: fill; prevade; inhabit; engross; busy; possess

OCCURRENCE: existence; circumstance; event; presence; appearance

ODD: unmatched; unequal; unusual; unique; eccentric; occasional

ODDS: difference; inequality; advantage; disagreement

(AT) ODDS: differing; disagreeing; at variance; dissentient; opposing; quarreling

ODDS (AND ENDS): remains; miscellany; refuse; mixture

ODIOUS: nasty; terrible; offensive; infamous; disreputable

OF: about; anent

OFF: odd; insane; occasional; dissonant; erroneous; imperfect; ill; tainted; unemployed; away

OFF (AND ON): irregularly; variably; by turns; to and fro

OFFEND: displease; affront; give umbrage

OFF (IT AND): careless; extemporaneous; informal; nonchalant

OFFENSE: violation; attack; umbrage; provocation; indignity; misdeed; illegality

OFFENSIVE: nasty; malodorous; combative; aggressive; odious; vulgar; ugly; insulting; obscene

OFFER: attempt; proffer; occur; adduce; bid

OFFICE: room; bureau; job; post; workplace; staff

OFFICIAL: functional; authentic; authoritative; officer

OFFSET: contrast; compensation; neutralizer; cushion; print

OFFSHOOT: addition; member; effect; byproduct; branch

OFTEN: repeatedly; frequently; over and over; again and again

OIL: lubricant; illuminant; lubricate; fat; balm; flattery; bribe; flatter; medicate

OILY: greasy; hypocritical; suave; flattering

OKAY (OK): correct; good; satisfactory; assent; approve; sanction; endorse; ratify; validate; authenticate; affirm; certify; pass; authorize; yes

OLD: ancient; mature; elderly; experienced; veteran

OMEN: portent; augury; auspice; presage; foretoken; preindication; sign; token; indication; promise; intimation; warning

OMISSION: deficiency; exlusion; error; neglect; want

ON: toward; forward; concerning; at; atop; upon

ONCE: whenever; former; single time

ONE: unit; person; an; identical; single

ONEROUS: ponderous; laborious; difficult; oppressive

ONE-SIDED: unilateral; distorted; prejudiced; partial

ONLY: merely; simply; solely; unique; alone

ONUS: impediment; imposition; duty

OOZE: seepage; mud; exude; reek; emit; filter; percolate

OPEN: unfasten; begin; convene; spread; unclose; unfold; disclose; persuasible; vacant; accessible; questionable; manifest; unprotected; unlimited; generous; honest; candid

OPENING: beginning; opportunity; vacancy; cleft; acupuncture; entranceway; outlet; admission; appearance; display; passageway; position

OPENLY: obviously; artlessly; outright

OPERATE: run; function; pilot; use; act

OPIATE: narcotic; drug; dope

OPINE: judge; think; suppose; remark

OPINION: belief; sentiment; feeling; impression; reaction; notion; idea; thought; view; concept; estimation; theory; assumption; judgment; advice

OPPONENT: adversary; antagonist; assailant; foe; enemy; rival; competitor; contestant; contender; disputant

OPPORTUNE: timely; appropriate; expedient

OPPOSE: counteract; refute; deny; resist

OPPOSITE: contrary; adverse; opposed

OPPOSITION: contrariety; counteraction; comparison; refutation; resistance; disapproval; at variance

OPPRESS: burden; persecute; tyrannize

OPPRESSIVE: stuffy; sultry; ponderous; tyrannical; distressing; depressing

OPTION: discretion; discrimination; pleasure; will; choice; alternative; dilemma

OR: optionally; either; alternatively

ORATION: speech; talk; discourse; address; recitation

ORBIT: sphere; circuit; route

ORDAIN: destine; enact; decree; appoint; allot; legalize

ORDERLY: attendant; uniform; arranged; regular; formal; peaceful

ORDINARILY: usually; frequently; plainly

ORDINARY: usual; average; frequent; prosaic; mediocre; vulgar; plain; plebeian

ORGANIZATION: composition; arrangement; classification; establishment; structure; association; sect

ORGANIZE: arrange; establish; classify

ORGY: spree; revel; debauch

ORIGINAL: fundamental; unimitated; beginning; characteristic; unconventional; new; novel; native; basic; genuine; inventive; unused

ORNERY: perverse; disobedient; malicious; ill-tempered

ORPHAN: waif; foundling; bereave; leave; bereft; parentless

OSCILLATE: fluctuate; vibrate; shake; generate; vacillate

OSTENSIBLE: apparent; plausible; illusory; specious; alleged

OUGHT: nothing; some; anything; must; should

OUST: eject; evict; depose

OUT: outlet; extinguish; divulge; odd; freed; escaped; absent; dislocated; exterior; unconscious; erroneous; minus; externally; away; forth; aloud

OUT (AT THE HEELS): solvenly; shabby; impoverished

OUTCAST: derelict; outlaw; abandoned; forlorn; forsaken; deserted; desolate; homeless; friendless

OUTCOME: effect; product; solution

OUTDO: excel; outwit; defeat

OUTFIT: wardrobe; equipment; costume; company; regiment; group

OUTLANDISH: unrelated; extraneous; barbarous; odd; impossible inelegant

OUTLAW: outcast; criminal; banish; ostracize

OUTLINE: contour; drawing; compendium; diagram; brief; summarize; describe; delineate

OUTLOOK: viewpoint; perspective; probability

OUT (OF THE WAY): farfetched; distant; devious; circuitous; secluded

OUTPOST: hinterland; environs; border; vanguard

OUTRAGE: mistreatment; evil; indignity; misdeed; mistreat; harm; offend; affront

OUTRAGEOUS: absurd; excessive; terrible; atrocious; unwarranted; exorbitant; disgraceful

OUTSTANDING: remaining; exterior; projecting; obvious; important; famous; due

OVER: superior; remaining; ended; done; past; beyond; higher; surplus; additionally; again; aloft; exceeding

OVERBOARD: excessive; immoderate; intemperate; extravagant; exorbitant; unwarranted; fancy; high; outrageous; preposterous; fabulous

OVERCOME: persuade; surmount; defeat; unnerve; overwrought; excite

OVERDUE: late; tardy; untimely; delayed; detained

OVERFED: oversized; overfull; satiated; gluttonous

OVERFLOW: abound; abundance; superabundance

OVERGROWN: overrun; oversize; luxuriant

OVERHAUL: inspection; audit; examine; repair

OVERLOOK: disregard; neglect; snub; condone; supervise; examine

OVERREACH: deceive; exceed; circumvent

OVERRIDE: overlap; conquer; tyrannize; annual

OVERRUN: pervade; spread; infest; overflow; abound; exceed

OVERTHROW: revolution; overturn; destruction; deposal; refute; destroy; defeat; depose; ruin

OVERTURN: revolution; inversion; destruction; defeat; capsize; refute; destroy;

OVERWHELM: submerge; inundate; refute; superabound; destroy; defeat; astonish; flood; excite; astound

P

PACE: walk; journey; measure
PACIFICISM: moderation; tranquility; peaceful; calmness; neutrality
PACK: arrange; prepare; squeeze; burden; assemblage
PACT: agreement; accord; understanding; treaty; contract; bargain; deal; negotiation
PAIN: suffering; sufferance; ache; smart; twinge; gripe; headache; discomfort; torment; torture; hurt; chafe; sting; bite; stab; grate; agonize; crucify; displeasure; discomfort; annoyance; irritation; plague; bother; vex; trouble; concern; grief; sorrow; affliction; unhappiness; misery; nightmare
PAINT: color; coat; deceive; delineate
PALE: dim; colorless; frightened; stake; limit; region
PALL: covering; mantle; insignia; funeral; disgust; dislike; weary; satiety
PALPABLE: material; tactile; obvious; manifest
PALPITATE: tremble; fear; color
PAMPER: endear; fondle; cherish; indulge
PANDEMONIUM: disorder; discord; turmoil; row; disturbance; tumult; uproar; riot; rumpus; fracas
PANEL: jury; partition; layer; list
PANIC: fear; apprehension; fearful; suspicion; nervousness; trepidation; alarmed; scared; afraid; breathless
PAR: equal; equivalence; similar; same
PARADOX: absurdity; obscurity; difficulty
PARAGON: perfect; glory; good (maw-woman)
PARALLEL: imitate; similarity; harmonious; symmetry; agree
PARAMOUNT: supreme; important; highest
PARE: cut; reduce; peel; shorten; divest
PARLEY: talk; conference; mediation
PARODY: copy; imitation; travesty; misrepresent; misinterpret
PAROLE: restrain; restrict; constrain; control
PAROXYSM: violence; agitation; emotion; anger
PARRY: defend; avert; confute
PART: role; duty; function; divide; portion; diverge; disjunction
PARTIAL: unequal; incomplete; unjust; biased
PARTIALITY: friendship; love; desire
PARTICIPATE: act; perform; perpetrate; exercise; proceed; cooperate; associate; concur; share; partake
PARTICULAR: item; event; careful; attentive; exact; fastidious
PARTISAN: friend; sympathizer; auxiliary
PARTNER: companion; friend; auxiliary; spouse; sharer

PARTY: person; association; assemblage; cooperate; agent; social; tea; outing; picnic

PASS: lapse; interval; happen; vanish; move; transfer; be superior; exceed; thrust; way; lane; egress; gratuity; annie-oakley; end; cease; die; neglect

PASS (OVER): exclude; cross; give; forgive; exemption

PASSABLE: small; unimportant; imperfect; pretty

PASSE: old; ancient; antiquated; obsolete; stale; outworn

PASSENGER: traveler; wayfarer; voyager; commuter; tourist

PASSION: emotion; pain; desire; love; anger

PASSIVE: inert; obedient; inactive; inexcitable

PASTE: glue; cement; attach; sham; tinsel

PAT ON THE BACK: endearment; strike; induce; comfort; approve; encourage

PATIENCE: perseverance; persistence; endurance; passiveness; tranquillity; calmness; meekness; tolerance

PATRON: customer; friend; benefactor

PATRONAGE: influence; protection; auspices; aid; assistance; furtherance; championship; favor; interest; advocacy

PAUCITY: small; few; scanty

PAUSE: cease; discontinue; quiescence; irresolution; doubt; repose

PAY: expend; defray; profitable; remunerate; punish; salary; wages; income

PEACE: amity; concord; silence; harmony; tranquillity; truce; calm; untroubled; still

PEACE OFFERING: gift; atonement; mediation; pacification

PEACOCK: beauty; proud; vain; gaudy

PEAK: height; summit; sharp

PEDAGOGUE: teacher; pedantic; scholar

PEEL: skin; layer; uncover; pare; separate

PEER: equal; pry; peek; peep; inquire; behold; search; look around

PEERLESS: supreme; glorious; virtuous; first rate

PELT: skin; dress; throw; attack; punish

PEN: write; restrain; imprison; enclose

PENALTY: punishment; retribution; fine; forfeit; sentence

PENCHANT: desire; love; willingness

PENITENTIARY: prison; jail; can; clink; reformatory; house of detention

PENSION: income; revenue; annuity; emolument

PEOPLE: kinfolk; inhabitants; mankind; laity; multitude

PERCEIVE: sensitive; conscious; impressionable; responsive; aware; see; behold; discern; discover; recognize; distinguish; copy; witness; know; comprehend; realize; understand; fathom

PERCH: height; support; location; abide; habitation

PEREMPTORY: assertion; firm; authoritative; rigorous; compulsory; duty

PERFECT: great; excellent; complete; entire; faultless; ideal; immaculate; impeccable; unblemished; best; inimitable; unparalleled
PERFORM: do; act; produce; achieve; fulfill
PERFUNCTORY: incomplete; sketchy; crude; hollow; meager; careless; remiss; slack
PERHAPS: possibly; maybe; perchance; peradventure; supposition; if; in case
PERIL: danger; insecurity; jeopardy; risk; hazard; liability; exposure; endanger; adventure; venture; threaten
PERIOD: end; termination; conclusion; finis; point; mark; term; time; duration; century; age
PERISH: disappear; die; annihilate; fall; destroy; decay
PERJURY: falsehood; mendacity; lie; prevarication; fabrication
PERMANENCE: durability; unchanging; unchangeable
PERMISSION: leave; allowance; sufferance; tolerance; liberty; license; concession; indulgence; favor; dispensation; exemption
PERMIT: let; allow; admit; suffer; tolerate; recognize; concede; accord; vouchsafe; favor; indulge; grant; empower; charter; enfranchise; license; authorize; warrant; sanction; patent
PERPETRATE: commit; inflect; action; excite; evolve
PERPETUAL: eternal; timeless; forever; everlasting; continual; constant; endless; unending; incessant; interminable; immortal; always
PERPLEX: bother; distract; derange; uncertainty
PERSECUTE: oppress; annoy; molest; abuse; outrage; injure
PERSEVERANCE: continuance; permanence; firmness; constancy; steadiness; persistence; stamina; pluck; game; backbone; grit
PERSIST: persevere; continue; durable; endure
PERSPECTIVE: view; outlook; vista; horizon; prospect; expectation; reckoning; calculation
PERSPIRATION: sweat; oozing; exudation
PERSUADE: induce; entice; attract; impress
PERSUASION: conviction; opinion; inducement; conception; belief; teaching
PERT: insolent; discourteous; vain
PETURBED: deranged; fermented; agitated; emotional; excited; fearful
PERUSE: study; read; learn
PERVADE: affect; extend; influence
PERVERSE: obstinate; difficult; sulky; churlish
PESTER: annoyer; annoyance; nuisance; aggrieve; vex; mortify; sicken; bore; bother; pother; plague
PET: flatter; fondle; favorite; love
PETITION: request; suit; prayer; requisition; demand; beseech; sue
PETRIFY: freeze; harden; dense; thrill; astonish; scare
PHASE: aspect; form; appearance; transition

PHILANTHROPY: altruism; benevolence; humanity; generosity; humanitarianism; cosmopolitanism; utilitarianism; public spirit

PHRASE: part; expression; sentence; paragraph; express; voice

PICK: axe; eat; select; choose; best; choice; finest; clean; censure; scold; extract; separate; destroy; find fault

PICKET: fence; guard; soldier; defense; join; torture; restrain; imprison; march; protest; demonstrate

PIECE: adjunct; bit; cannon; drama; courtesan; flap; label; tag; strip; tail; part

PIERCE: perforate; wound; hurt; affect

PIERCING: loud; shrill; cold; feeling

PILE: heap; edifice; stake; post; wealth; accumulation; lump; lot; batch

PILFER: steal; thieve; rob; purloin; filch; lift; palm

PILOT: aviator; mariner; director; inform; guide; lead

PIN: fasten; fastening; nail; rivet; locate; establish; fix; root; sharp; needle; axis; axle; spindle; pivot; trifle; trivial

PINCH: hurt; pain; chill; contract; emergency; difficulty; need; adversity

PIONEER: precursor; leader; teacher; prepare

PIPE: tube; conduit; vent; weep; sound; cry

PIRATE: privateer; buccaneer; brigand; thief; plagiarist; pillager; marauder; corsair; steal; thieve; rob; pilfer; plagiarize

PIT: hole; opening; grave; extract

PITCH: degree; locate; erect; throw; reel; toss; summit; height; tar; black; resin

PITCH INTO: attack; contend; punish

PITCH UPON: reach; discover; choose; get

PITH: gist; meaning; center; interior; strength

PITIABLE: bad; contemptible; painful

PITIFUL: unimportant; bad; disrepute

PIVOT: axis; junction; support; cause

PLACARD: manifesto; advertisement; bill; broadside; poster; notice

PLACE: locate; location; abode; office; rank; order; arrange; situation; circumstance

PLAGIARISM: piracy; theft; borrowing; imitation

PLAGUE: pain; bore; annoy; pest; bother; pother; nuisance; grievance

PLAIN: obvious; manifest; horizontal; simple; artless; ugly

PLAINT: cry; vociferation; outcry; clamor; lamentation; wail; complaint; murmur; mutter; grumble; whine

PLAINTIFF: accuser; complainant; petitioner

PLAN: scheme; representation; information; itinerary

PLANE: horizontal; flat; smooth; fly; soar

PLANT: place; sow; insert; trick; factory

PLASTER: cement; repair; remedy; cover

PLATFORM: dais; stage; arena; support; scheme; horizontal

PLAY: amusement; game; operation; drama; influence; scope; use
(FALSE) PLAY: deception; deceive; disappoint; lie
PLAY FAST AND LOOSE: lie; irresolute; caprice
PLEA: defense; argument; excuse; vindication
PLEAD: argue; beg; plea
PLEASANT: agreeable; amusing; witty; flattering; inducing
PLEDGE: affirmation; promise; security; borrow
PLENTY: multitude; numerous; profusion; scores; many; several; sundry; sufficient; adequate; enough
PLIANT: soft; facile; servile; irresolute
PLUCK: resolution; perseverence; courage; take; steal
PLUNGE: dive; immerse; insert; hurry
PLUS: addition; increase; add; supplement; extra
POINT: small; speck; end; mark; place; topic; intention
(MAKE A) POINT OF: contention; resolution; compulsion; condition
POINTED: sharp; marked; concise; affirmation
POLISH: smooth; rub; furbish; ornament; politeness; taste
POLITIC: wise; cunning; cautious
POLLUTE: stain; sully; defile; debase; contaminate; taint
PONDER: deliberate; speculate; study; meditate
POOR: weak; insufficient; trifling; indigent
POPULAR: celebrated; favorite; approved; in demand
PORTION: part; piece; cut; chunk; slice; share; split; dividend; allotment; measure
POSITION: proposition; assertion; circumstances
POSITIVE: real; great; certain; strict; unequivocal; obstinate; absolute
POST: fasten; support; situation; location; beat; mail; transmit; record; position; job; stigmatize; punish
POTENT: valid; powerful; able; capable; strong; mighty; vigorous; influence; potential; capability; authority
PRAISE: approbation; approval; sanction; estimation; esteem; admiration; admire; kudos; commendation; laud; encomium; homage; applause; plaudit; cheer; value; prize; honor; compliment
PRATE: palaver; chatter; prattle; jabber
PRECARIOUS: dangerous; uncertain; transient
PRECAUTION: care; safety; preparation; expedient
PRECEPT: adage; maxim; order; permit
PRECIOUS: great; excellent; valuable; beloved
PRECOCIOUS: pert; rude; immature
PREDOMINANT: dominant; prevalent; important; influential; paramount; supreme; preponderant
PREFACE: precede; introduce; prelude; prefix; preliminary; preamble; prologue; forward; lead; heading
PREJUDICE: disadvantage; drawback; harmful; injurious; evil; detriment; adulterate; prejudge; misjudgment; presume; presuppose;

bias; partial; one-sidedness; intolerance; opinionated; bigoted; obstinacy

PREMATURE: early; precipitation; anticipation; beforehand; hastily

PREMEDITATION: predetermination; predeliberation; well-laid; well-devised; deliberately; intentionally; design; purpose; contemplation; knowingly

PREMISE: prefix; precede; announcement; precursor; prior; evidence; logic

PREPARE: facilitate; smooth; disencumber; free; clear; ready; anticipate; expect

PREPOSTEROUS: absurd; ridiculous; exaggerated; undue

PRESCRIBE: direct; advise; order; enjoin

PRESENT: here; now; existing; occupying; inhabitating; offer; give; proffer; tender; propose; volunteer; bestow; donate; deliver; endow; award; dispense; confer; furnish

PRESS: iron; crowd; move; compel; offer; solicit; communications; medium; print; attack; drive

PRESSURE: power; influence; weight; urgency; exertion; adversity

PRESTIGE: repute; distinction; character; notable; fame; renown; popularity; esteem; glory; honor; illustriousness; respect; distinguished; celebrated

PRESUME: hope; suppose; believe; misjudge

PRESUMPTION: probability; supposition; expectation; arrogance; rashness

PRETENCE: excuse; boast; falsehood; ostentation; imitation

PRETEND: assert; simulate; deceive; brag

PRETENTIOUS: vain; affected; boasting; ostentatious

PREVAIL: exist; live; current; rife; predominate; influence; persuade; press; prompt; sway; succeed; triumph

PREVENT: hinder; obstruct; stop; prohibit; impede; retard; interfere; bar; thwart; foil

PREVIOUS: before; prior; earlier; already

PRICE: consideration; equivalent; change; money; value; rate; worth; cost; amount; charge; figure; expense; appraise; reward

PRIM: affected; fastidious; proud

PRIME: important; excellent; early; prepared; teach

PRINCELY: famous; noble; liberal; generous

PRINCIPLE: rule; element; tenet; maxim; reasoning; idea; cause; motive; intrinsic

PRIOR: preceding; anterior; before; former; previous; earlier; in anticipation

PRIVATE: soldier; G.I.; special; hidden; secluded

PRIVILEGE: permission; exemption; freedom

PRIZE: gain; booty; reward; receipt; approve; love

PROBE: perforator; investigate; inquire; request; search; quest;

examine; review; scrutinize; explore; sift; calculate; analyze; question; study

PROBLEM: topic; question; enigma

PRODUCE: fruit; merchandise; cause; effect; create; show; stage

PROFILE: outline; silhouette; sideways; face; feature; protract

PROFOUND: deep; leaned; wise; great; sagacious

PROFUSION: numerous; plenty; multitude; host; array

PROGRAM: plan; design; project; prospectus; publication; catalog

PROJECT: program; plan; scheme; design; impel; throw; fling; pitch; toss; hurl

PROLIFIC: productive; teeming; fertile

PROLONG: continue; lengthen; protract

PROMINENT: important; notable; signal; salient; paramount; foremost; significant; eminent; famous; renowned; popular; distinguished; noted

PROMPT: early; on time; cue; tell; remind; advise; induce; motivate; activate

PRONOUNCE: advance; allege; express; propose; propound; enunciate; broach; contend; maintain; speak; utter; deliver

PROPITIOUS: timely; beneficial; auspicious; helping

PROPOSE: suggest; broach; intend; offer

PROPOSITION: supposition; reasoning; suggestion; offer; project

PROSCRIBE: condemn; interdict; banish; curse

PROSECUTE: pursue; act; accuse; arraign

PROSTRATE: horizontal; low; dejected; exhausted; depressed; servile; powerless; destroyed

PROTEST: dissent; assert; declare; profess; deny; contradict; refuse; disclaim; deprecate; expostulate; retract; repudiate; nullify

PROVIDENT: careful; prepared; wise

PROVOKE: incite; excite; vex; anger; cause

PROXY: substitute; deputy; alternate; understudy; representative

PRUDENT: careful; wise; cautious; economical

PUERILE: foolish; trifling; boyish; feeble

PUFF: wind; inflate; pant; flatter; praise; boast; exaggerate; advertisement

PULL: advantage; odds; influence; row; scull; paddle; draw; haul; lug; drag

PULL TO PIECES: separate; destroy; detract; censure

PULL UP: stop; rest; accuse; reprimand

PUN: alliteration; rhyme; joke; ambiguity; double entendre; jest

PUNCH: strike; vigor; perforate; engrave; beverage

PUNCTILIOUS: exact; observant; scrupulous; ostentatious

PUNCTUAL: early; on time; exact; observing; scrupulous

PUPPET: effigy; dupe; tool; auxiliary

PURE: clean; artless; virtuous; innocent; chaste; simple; true; honorable; devout

PURGE: expel; shed; banish; overthrow; oust; empty; drain; sweep out; extract; clean; expurgate; atone; shrive; absolve

PURPOSE: intention; project; undertaking; design; ambition; object; aim; end; goal; target; mean

PUSH: impel; propel; essay; progress; activity; haste; exigency; eject

PUT: place; locate; set; lodge; stow; lay; station; quarter; post; install; situate; embed; esconce; root; moor

PUT ASIDE: exclude; neglect; disuse; inattentive

PUT DOWN: destroy; conquer; compel; pay; humiliate; record

Q

QUACK: charlatan; imposter; pretender; humbug; fraud; faker; phony; cry; call; honk

QUAIL: recoil; cringe; wince; flinch; cower

QUAKE: shake; vibrate; tremble; quiver; shiver; shudder

QUALIFICATION: limitation; allowance; discount; extenuation; training; fitness; talent; eligibility; preparation

QUALIFIED: limited; modified; eligible; competent; entitled

QUALITY: nature; characteristic; atmosphere; capacity; excellence; nobility

QUALM: doubt; apprehension; demur

QUANDARY: dilemma; perplexity; paradox

QUARANTINE: isolation; confinement; isolate; segregrate; separate; seclude; confine

QUARREL: dispute; controversy; altercation; fight; squabble; contention; bicker; wrangle; scrap; hassle; spat; row; feud; fuss; rhubarb; disagree; differ

QUARTER: coin; fourth; semester; region; clemency; house

(GIVE NO) QUARTER: show no mercy; turn a deaf ear

(GIVE) QUARTER: have pity; have mercy upon; melt; thaw; relent; relax

QUASH: extinguish; suppress; hush up; whitewash

QUASI: like; imitation; seemingly; as if

QUAVER: quiver; tremble; trepidation; shake; excited; afraid

QUEENLY: noble; dignified; regal

QUEER: counterfeit; disable; spoil; thwart; odd; insane; eccentric; false; homosexual; fairy; pansy; bisexual; queen

QUELL: calm; extinguish; suppress; subdue; temper

QUENCH: extinguish; discourage; destroy; suppress; gratify

QUERY: question; inquiry; interrogation; problem; contention

QUEST: search; hunt; rummage

QUESTION: topic; query; doubt; problem

(OUT OF THE) QUESTION: impossible; rejected; refused; prohibited; hopeless

QUESTIONABLE: unbelievable; improbable; doubtful; deceptive; dishonest

QUESTIONNAIRE: canvas; survey; inquiry; poll

QUEUE: afterpart; hair; tail; line

QUIBBLE: cavil; bicker; quip; quirk; dodge; sidestep; pussyfoot; equivocate; prevaricate; parry; fence; hedge; evasion

QUICK: vital part; sore spot; sudden; prompt; fast; alert; lively; hasty; impulsive; smart; teachable; dextrous; hot-tempered

QUICKEN: energize; accelerate; refresh; hasten; facilitate; further; stimulate

QUIET: silence; peace; calm; gentle; peaceful; inexcitable; modest; tasteful; composed

QUINTESSENCE: essence; best; perfection; extract

QUIP: eccentricity; caprice; quibble; gibe; witticism; joke; jest; wisecrack; pun

QUIRK: mannerism; eccentricity; witticism; caprice; quibble; twist

QUIT: separate; cease; depart; go; abandon; resign; dispose; discard; clear; free; rid

QUITE: somewhat; very; positively; absolutely; yes

QUIVER: sheath; agitation; flicker; tremolo; excitement; fear; trepidation; nervous; shake; shiver

QUI VIVE: alert; attentive; awake; excited; ready; smart; keen; sharp

QUIZ: examination; test; trial; oral; inquiry; interrogation; questioning

QUOTA: portion; share; part; proportion; percentage; measure; ratio; rate

QUOTE: repeat; reproduce; duplicate; cite; name; call; exemplify; illustrate

R

RABBLE: mob; force; crowd; ragtag; the ruck; the rout

RABBLE ROUSER: demagogue; ringleader; agitator; fomenter; inflamer; inciter; provoker

RABID: mad; fantical; infuriated; overwrought

RACE: people; speed; accelerate; compete; flow; stream

RACIAL: tribal; national; family; clan; lineal; ethnic; genetic

RACK: pain; strain; torment; punish; ruin

RACKET: noise; commotion; fraud; vocation; bat

RACKETEER: gangster; criminal; felon; crook; lawbreaker

RADIANCE: radiation; light; beauty; cheerfulness

RADIANT: shining; cheerful; beautiful; illustrious; beaming

RADICAL: extremist; reformer; essential; extreme; thorough; original; basic; vital

RAG: cloth; garment; dress; banter; berate; shoddy

(IN) RAGS: slovenly; shabby; impoverished

RAGE: turbulence; frenzy; craze; fad; excitement; anger; prevail; blow; bluster; storm

RAGING: turbulent; storming; rabid; overwrought; infuriated; blustering

RAID: attack; pillage; plunder

RAISE: increase; promotion; assemble; rear; construct; erect; emboss; elevate; grow; train; promote; excite; provoke; glorify; conjure

RALLY: assemblage; recovery; arrange; form; call; assemble; improve; recover; banter; ridicule

RAMBLE: wander; digress; deviated; wandering; delirious

RAMPANT: prevalent; unruly; abundant; unrestrained

RANCOR: animosity; malevolence; resentment; revengefulness

RANDOM: haphazardly; casually; orderless

RANGE: mountain; series; rank; size; distance; direction; scale; scope; arrange; extend; wander; search; oven; stove

RANK: character; grade; class; series; prestige; nobility; arrange; classify; precede; range; size; assess; coarse; unsavory; malodorous; bad; foul; tainted; wicked; indecent; filthy; terrible

RAPPORT: relationship; agreement; empathy; accord

RARE: unsubstantial; unusual; sparse; infrequent; thin; undercooked; scarce; notable

RASP: abrade; chafe; irritate; grind; file

RATE: rank; ratio; velocity; price; quantify; classify; measure; assess; deserve; berate

RATHER: contrarily; somewhat; however; instead; preferably

RATIONAL: intelligent; sane; reasonable; practical

RATTLE: racket; noisemaker; clatter; percussive; fluster; nonsense; chatter

RAVAGE: infestation; devestation; pillage; debauch; infest; plunder; ruin; destroy

RAVE: enthuse; bluster; be insane; be violent

RAVING: turbulent; rabid; overwrought; infuriated; blustering; beautiful

RAVISHING: alluring; delightful; beautiful

RAW: immature; naked; nude; cold; sore; ignorant; undeveloped; unprepared; inexperienced; vulgar; indecent

RAZE: level; fell; obliterate; demolish

REACH: equal; influence; extend; arrive; overtake; bribe; deliver

REACTION: effect; response; opinion; resistance

REACTIONARY: conservative; recalcitrant; malcontent; counteractive; reactive; apostate

REACTIVATE: re-engergize; restore; remilitarize

READ: peruse; recite; interpret; understand

READILY: willingly; eagerly; quickly; easily

READY: train; fix; repair; alert; willing; eager; prepared

REALLY: actually; positively; truly; literally

REAR: back; posterior; rump; loom; produce; construct; rise; erect; raise; grow; train

REASON: cause; intellect; sensibleness; sanity; logic; solution; explanation; motive; justification; rationalize; discuss; deduce

REASONABLE: moderate; sane; logical; practical; inexpensive; justifiable

REASSURE: comfort; embolden; give hope

REBEL: revolutionist; insurgent; revolt; rise; mutiny

REBUFF: repulse; reject; defeat; refuse; resist; snub

REBUKE: reprimand; reproach; reprehension; scold; chide; upbraid; admonish

RECALCITRANT: reactionary; ungovernable; disobedient; resistant

RECALL: repeal; remember; recent; summon

RECEPTIVE: pliant; sensory; sensible; persuasible; openminded

RECESS: pause; nook; indentation; refuge; respite; adjourn; rest

RECIPROCATE: correspond; interchange; alternate; concur; retaliate

RECITAL: concert; speech; narration; reiteration

RECKLESS: careless; rash; unconcerned

RECOGNIZE: see; know; detect; acknowledge

RECOGNIZED: traditional; known; acknowledged; conventional

RECOMMEND: advocate; vouch; urge; advise

RECOMPENSE: compensation; restitution; remuneration; atonement; pay

RECONCILIATION: pacification; adjustment; conformity

RECRUIT: newcomer; novice; conscript; draft; reinforce; replenish; restore

RECTIFY: adjust; straighten; refine; amend; remedy

RECURRENT: repeated; frequent; periodic; habitual

REDEEM: convert; substitute; reclaim; rescue; recover; pay; atone; fulfill

REDRESS: reparation; restitution; recompence; reprisal; atonement; remedy

REDUCE: decrease; weaken; dilute; moderate; shorten; abridge; slenderize; lower; conquer; subdue; denote; impoverish; cheapen; abase; relieve; diminish; depreciate; humble

REEL: whirl; sway; flounder; rotate

REFER: relate; attribute; cite; indicate

REFINED: fine; rare; discriminative; precise; meticulous; perfected; purified; fastidious; tasteful; well bred; elegant; improved; cultivated

REFLECTION: duplicate; reaction; light; reverberation; thought; idea; recollection; image; remark; aspersion; criticism

REFORM: amend; convert; reproduce; remake; regenerate

REFUTE: confute; rebut; parry; answer; dismiss; contradict; oppose; deny

REGALE: treat; feed; refresh; gratify; amuse; entertain

REGARD: observe; aspect; attitude; attention; care; repute; consideration; respect; relevance; contemplate; judge; think; heed; obey

REGARDLESS: inattentive; careless; unconcerned; notwithstanding; anyhow

REGENERATE: convert; reproduce; revive; redeem; save

REGULAR: uniform; orderly; usual; constant; habitual

REGULATE: adjust; organize; influence; remedy; govern; manage; prescribe; legislate

REINFORCE: intensify; add; strengthen; replenish; restore

REJECT: exclude; expel; repudiate; discard; refuse; disapprove

RELATE: associate; correlate; report; state; narrate

RELAX: slacken; soften; rest; ease up; slow down

RELEASE: news item; radio broadcast; demobilize; death; escape; rescue; exemption; liberation; relinquishment; receipt; relief; acquittal; dismiss; free

RELEGATE: exclude; banish; discard; consign

RELENT: moderate; pity; yield; submit

RELENTLESS: persevering; unyielding; strict; merciless

RELIABLE: stable; sure; safe; solvent; trustworthy

RELIEVE: lighten; cure; help; ease

RELINQUISH: release; surrender; abandon

RELY: trust; confide; depend; rest; repose; hope

REMARKABLE: great; extraordinary; notable; wonderful

REMISS: dilatory; negligent; reluctant; indolent

REMOTE: farfetched; distant; reserved; haughty; unsociable; secluded

REMOVE: deduct; disjoin; eliminate; divert; doff; depart; extract; eject; dismiss; evacuate; discard; eradicate; depose; relieve

REMOVED: unrelated; alone; distant; reserved; secluded

RENDER: do; execute; give; pay; narrate; communicate; translate

RENOUNCE: deny; recant; abandon; reject

REPARATION: remedy; repair; restitution; recompense; atonement

REPLACE: substitute; supplant; discharge; restore

REPLY: epistle; retaliation; defense; react; reverberate; answer

REPORT: critique; verdict; information; rumor; publication; accounting; commentary; account; response; relate; announce; narrate

REPRESENT: exhibit; delineate; typify; describe; enact; pretend; picture

REPUDIATE: exclude; deny; recant; reject

REPUGNANT: contrary; disagreeing; counteractive; nasty; denying; opposed; resistant; odious; ugly; hostile

REPULSE: snub; resist; refuse; reject; repel; defeat

REQUIRE: entail; necessitate; lack; demand; oblige; charge

RESCIND: repeal; revoke; reverse; abrogate; retract; recall; cancel; annul

RESCUE: deliverance; extrication; release; liberation; recovery; save; redeem; free; emancipate; help

RESOLUTE: determined; perseverant; obstinate; unyielding; bold

RESPITE: delay; pause; rest; reprieve
REST: remainder; pause; support; stair; calm
(AT) REST: quiescent; dead; buried; abed; comfortable; anchored
RESTLESS: changeable; agitated; excited; bustling; wakeful; fidgety; impatient
RESTRAIN: moderate; limit; qualify; hinder; constrain; confine
RESTRAINT: moderation; limitation; elegance; reserve; inhibition; constraint; equanimity; tastefulness; modesty; temperance
RETIRE: retreat; recede; depart; discharge; depose; resign; go to bed
RETORT: answer; repartee; retaliation; recrimination
RETREAT: recoil; depart; recede; depart; seclusion; refuge
RETRENCH: reduce; curtail; economize
RETROGRESS: revert; regress; deteriorate
RETURN: repetition; reversion; reaction; regression; retort; recovery; relapse; restitution; repayment; retaliation; answer; repeat; recur; revert; revive; yield; resume; revisit
REVEAL: open; discover; manifest; disclose; indicate
REVERSE: opposite; reversion; inversion; backup; relapse; defeat; repeal; contradictory; backward
REVIEW: parade; reiteration; reconsideration; discussion; inspection; critique; magazine; commentary; discuss; examine; remember; relate
REVILE: curse; berate; ridicule
REVIVE: remember; restore; recover; refresh
REVOLT: revolution; rebellion; disapproval; strike; dissent; offend; rebel; revolutionize; resist; disobey; shock
RIBALD: vulgar; impure; disreputable
RICH: savory; abundant; wealthy; beautiful
RICKETY: weak; ugly; imperfect
RID: deliver; liberate; loosen; relinquish
RIDICULOUS: absurd; foolish; trifling; grotesque
RIGHT: dextral; straight; true; just; privilege; virtuous
RIGID: hard; exact; severe; regular
RING: combination; clique; resonance; sound; loud; circle; fastening; pendency
RIOT: confusion; derangement; violence; discord; resist; mutiny
RISE: grow; begin; stir; revolt; ascend; progress; slope
RISK: danger; chance; invest
RISQUE: loose; suggestive; coarse; broad; free; equivocal; smutty; ribald; obscene; bawdy; pornographic
RITE: ceremony; ordinance; observance; function; duty; sacrament; incantation; service; ritual; rubric; canon
RIVAL: opponent; combatant; emulate; oppose; outshine
ROAR: violence; wind; sound; bellow; laugh; weep
ROBBER: thief; pilferer; rifler; filcher; plagiarist; brigand; bandit; thug; plunderer; racketeer; highwayman; footpad; crook; burglar
ROBBERY: stealing; theft; thievery; appropriation; plagiarism; hold

up; foray; purloining; pilfering; filching; lifting

ROGUE: cheat; knave; scamp

ROLL: list; record; convolution; rotundity; rotate; rock; flow; fly; move; smooth; sound

ROOT: cause; origin; source; principle; element; rudiment; embryo; nucleus; stem; establish; locate; fix; pin; base; basis; etymon

ROSTER: list; panel; enumeration; register; record; census; roll

ROT: decompose; putrefy; decay; disease; absurdity; rubbish

ROTTEN: weak; bad; foul; decayed; diseased; deceptive

ROUGH: eneven; shapeless; violent; ugly; churlish; sour; unsavory; pungent; unprepared; bully; uncouth; artless; vulgar

ROUND: rotund; curve; circle; series; revolution

(COME) ROUND: recant; persuade

(TURN) ROUND: revolve; invert; retreat

ROUTINE: uniform; order; rule; custom

ROW: disorder; discord; violence; series; tier; street; navigate

RUB: friction; abrasion; erase; touch; knead; massage; brush; graze; contact; difficulty; trial; emergency; adversity; cross; check; misfortune

RUBBISH: garbage; absurdity; useless; trifling; unmeaning

RUDE: violent; ugly; vulgar; uncivil; uncivilized; disrespectful; shapeless; inelegant; ignorant

RUE: regret; deplore; bewail; lament; repent

RUFFIAN: scoundrel; blusterer; maleficent

RUFFLE: disorder; derange; roughen; fold; excite; anger; pain

RUGGED: shapeless; rough; difficult; ugly

RUIN: destroy; destruction; evil; failure; adversity; poverty

RULE: meaning; custom; precept; law; measure; line; regularity; govern; influence; decide

RUMPLE: disorder; derange; roughen; fold

RUMPUS: discord; confusion; violence

RUN: speed; motion; flow; liquefy; sequence; repetition; continuance; generality; habit; eventuality; course; score

RUN AMUCK: kill; attack; mad; violent

RUN DOWN: underestimate; pursue; bad; finished; attack; depreciate; detract

RUN RIOT: active; disobey; intemperance; violent; exaggerate; redundance

RUSH: haste; velocity; violence; crowd

RUSTY: dirty; decayed; sluggish; unskilled

RUT: habitually; uniformly; hackneyed; fixed; rooted; inveterate; ingrained; customary; traditional; usual; ordinary; common; familiar; trite; commonplace; stereotyped

RUTHLESS: savage; revengeful; pitiless

S

SABOTAGE: destroy; disrupt; disorganize; ravage; devastate

SACK: bag; plunder; discharge

SACRED: dignified; consecrated; enshrined; glorified; exalted; sacrosanct; heroic; sublime; solemn; august; stately; worshipful; holy; hallowed; heavenly; seraphic

SACRIFICE: gift; oblation; offering; benefaction; favor; destroy; atonement; scapegoat

SACRILEGE: impiety; profanity; irreverence; sacrilegious; blasphemy

SACROSANCT: honorable; holy; inviolable

SAD: painful; sore; bitter; piteous; grieving; miserable; cruel; woeful; lamenting; shocking; frightful; dreadful; terrible; horrible; distressed; baleful; gray; drab; dingy; wretched; bad; deplorable; affliction; dejected; melancholy; pensive

SAFE: container; chest; strongbox; secreted; screened; covered; secured; invulnerable; protected; guarded; sheltered; snug; impregnable; preserved; prudent; cautious; discreet; politic

SAGE: wise; sapient; sagacious; rational; sound; sensible; judicious

SAID: stated; repeated; orated; iterated; reiterated; asserted; parroted; echoed; spoken

SALAAM: bow; courtesy; respect; submit

SALARY: compensation; remuneration; allowance; wages; stipend

SALIENT: important; manifest; sharp; projecting

SALUTE: courtesy; respect; kiss; celebrate

SALVO: explosion; attack; excuse; exception; plea; qualification

SANCTION: permission; let; allow; admit; approbation; approval; advocate; authority; warranty; charter

SANCTUARY: refuge; retreat; stronghold; asylum; haven; shelter; shrine; altar; sanctum-sanctorum; sacristy

SAP: essence; juice; excavate; destroy; damage; attack

SARCASM: disrespect; irony; disparagement; affront; insult; mockery; rudeness; derisiveness; contempt; censure; insinuation; innuendo; caricature; ridicule

SARCASTIC: satirica; sardonic; cynical; dry; sharp; cutting; biting; severe; virulent; withering; trenchant; ironical; caustic; acrimonious

SATANIC: malevolent; vicious; diabolic

SATELLITE: servant; auxiliary; heavenly body; companion; follower

SATISFY: answer; convince; suffice; consent; observe; pay; gratify; content; reward; satiate

SAVAGE: violent; angry; malevolent; vulgar; boorish

SAVE: except; exclude; store; preserve; economize

SCANDAL: detraction; disparagement; vilification; obloguy; scurrility;

defamation; traducement; slander; calumny; libel

SCANT: small; few; little; insufficient; narrow

SCAR: blemish disfigurement; deformity; defeat; flaw; injury; bruise; stain

SCATTER: derange; dispense; diverge; confute; destroy

SCHISM: dissent; discord; heterodoxy

SCOFF: ridicule; deride; despise; censure

SCOPE: degree; extent; meaning; opportunity

SCORE: count; list; twenty; notch; mark; debt; success; motive

SCOWL: complain; disapprobation; frown; sullen; anger

SCRAMBLE: climb; confusion; pursue; contend; seize; haste

SCRAPE: abrade; reduce; pulverize; difficulty; mischance

SCRATCH: mark; mar; groove; abrade; daub; draw; write; hunt; wound

SCREEN: sift; sieve; filter; clean; movies; cinema; shade; hide; shelter; defense; defend

SCRUBBY: small; trifling; stingy; disreputable; vulgar; shabby

SCRUPULOUS: careful; incredulous; exact; fastidious

SEAL: close; complete; resolve; matrix; mark; compact; secure

SEARCH: inquire; look; research; quest; investigate; question; explore; study; reconnoiter; examine; seek; peer; pry; hunt; track; trail; shadow

SECTION: division; part; chapter; class

SECURE: fasten; tie; restrain; engage; confident; safe; gain; get

SEDATE: calm; grave; thoughtful

SEE: view; look; know; believe; attend

SEEDY: diseased; deteriorated; exhausted; needy

SEEK: ask; inquire; request; pursue

SEGREGATE: detach; separate; part; divide; disunite; cut off; exclude; relegate; bar

SEMBLANCE: similarity; probability; imitation; copy; appearance

SEND: transfer; delegate; consign; mail; post; ship; propel; fire off; let off; eject

SENSATION: impression; effect; emotion; feeling; rapture; titillation; wonder; marvel

SENSELESS: absurd; foolish; unmeaning; insensible

SEPARATE: disjoin; disect; exclude; divorce; select; discriminate

SERENE: placid; calm; content; imperturbable

SERIOUS: resolved; important; dejected

SET: cohere; join; class; group; gang; place; prepare; firm; stage

SET AGAINST: oppose; quarrel; hate; angry; disapprove

SET ASIDE: displace; disregard; neglect; reject; annul; relinquish

SET OUT: arrange; display; decorate; depart; begin

SET AT REST: complete; end; answer; adjudge

SET RIGHT: inform; disclose; teach; reinstate; vindicate

SET UP: originate; produce; strengthen; raise; upright; successful; prosperous

160

SET DOWN: record; unseat; humiliate; slight; censure

SETTLE: locate; establish; pay; regulate; decide; choose; consent; subside; moderate; end

SEVERE: exact; harsh; painful; critical

SHABBY: trifling; deteriorated; stingy; mean; disgraceful

SHACKLE: fasten; tie; fetter; hinder; restrain

SHADE: degree; darkness; shadow; color; conceal; screen; surpass

SHADOW: unsubstantial; small; thin; accompaniment; dark; shade; pursue

SHAKE: totter; vibrate; shiver; thrill; weak; excited; injure; dissuade; fear

SHAKE HANDS: courtesy; forgive; pacification; friendship

SHAKE THE HEAD: deny; refuse; dissent; disapprove

SHALLOW: ignorant; foolish; trifling

SHAM: deception; falsehood; lie; imitation

SHAMELESS: bold; impudent; indecent

SHARP: energetic; violent; acute; pungent; intelligent; active; clever; cunning; painful; rude

SHAVE: reduce; shorten; cut; smooth

SHED: building; scatter; divest; give; emit

SHELVE: defer; neglect; disuse

SHIFT: change; convert; substitute; move; transfer

SHOCK: violence; concussion; agitation; discord; affect; move; pain; scandalize

SHOCKING: bad; painful; ugly; vulgar; disreputable; fearful

SHOOT: dart; propel; kill; execute; pain; offspring; sprout

SHORT: concise; uncivil; inferior; insufficient; small; incomplete

SHOW: visible; appear; evidence; demonstrate; manifest; parade; disclose

SHOW FIGHT: defy; attack; defend; bravery

SHOW UP: visible; manifest; ridicule; degrade; censure; accuse

SHOWY: fashionable; vulgar; ostentatious

SHREWD: knowing; wise; cunning

SHRINK: decrease; shrivel; withdraw; avoid

SHUFFLE: mix; derange; change; interchange; agitate; prepare

SHUT: unopened; close; occlude; plug; block; stop; dam; obturate; seal

SHY: deviate; avoid; fearful; cowardly; modest; cautious

SICKEN: nauseate; pain; weary; disgust

SIFT: clean; sort; simplify; inquire; discriminate

SIGN: attest; write; record; omen; indication

SIGNIFY: mean; inform; forebode

SILENCE: disable; check; confute; conceal; soundless; latency

SIMMER: agitate; excite; boil

SIMPLE: mere; unmixed; silly; ignorant; artless; unadorned

SINK: disappear; destroy; descend; lower; submerge; fail; invest

SIZE: degree; magnitude; dimension

SKETCH: form; paint; represent; describe; plan
SKULL: head; pate; noodle; pericranium; cerebrum; cranium
SLACK: loose; weak; inert; slow; neglectful; inactive; lax; moderate.
SLAP: strike; censure; punish; oppose; attack; disrespect
SLENDER: small; thin; trifling; slight
SLIGHT: small; slender; rare; neglect; disparage; feeble; trifle; disrespect; contempt
SLIP: small; lapse; descend; error; fail
SLIPPERY: smooth; greasy; uncertain; dangerous; facile
SLOVENLY: untidy; careless; dirty; awkward; vulgar
SLOW: tardy; inert; moderate; wearisome; dull
SLUR: blemish; stigma; reproach; glossover
SMACK: kiss; thud; strike; taste; small quantity; savor
SMALL: little; tiny; minute; weeny; fine; dribbling; paltry; faint; slender; slight; scant; limited; few; meager; sparce; petty; shallow; insufficient
SMART: pain; feel; grief; clever; witty; pretty
SMEAR: cover; stain; soil; defile; spot; dirty; tarnish; daub; smudge; sully; debase; blemish
SMOKE: dust; vapor; heat; dirt; cigarette; cigar; cure; unimportant
SMOTHER: repress; kill; stifle; restrain
SNEAK: coward; knave; base; servile; hide
SNUB: slur; humiliate; bluster; censure; hinder; short
SNUG: secluded; contented; safe; comfortable; closed
SOAK: immerse; water; moisten; drunkard
SOBER: moderate; wise; sane; grave; temperate; abstinent; calm; humble
SOFT: weak; moderate; smooth; moist; dulcet; lenient; tender; timid
SOFTEN: moderate; pity; relieve; palliate
SOLICITUDE: care; pain; anxiety; desire
SOLID: complete; dense; certain; exact; solvent; wise; learned
SOMBER: dark; black; gray; sad
SOOTHE: allay; relieve; flatter
SOUND: stable; strong; noise; measure; investigate; true; wise; sane; good; perfect; healthy; solvent
SOUR: acid; discontented; embitter; uncivil; sulky
SPAN: join; link; time; transient; distance; near; short; measure; length
SPARE: extra; small; meager; refrain; scanty; disuse; relinquish; give; economize; exempt; temperate; parsimonious
SPASMODIC: discontinuous; irregular; changeable; violent
SPECTACLE: appearance; phenomenon; sight; show; scene; display; drama
SPECULATE: view; think; suppose; chance; essay; traffic; experiment
SPEND: effuse; expend; purchase; give; waste
SPHERE: domain; space; region; world; ball; rank

SPILL: splash; waste; lavish; shed
SPIRIT: essence; meaning; courage; ghost
SPIRITED: active; brave; cheerful; generous; sensitive
SPLASH: affuse; stream; spatter; display; fame; parade
SPLIT: divide; disect; quarrel; apportion
SPOIL: vitiate; hinder; plunder; deface; satiate; booty
SPOKESMAN: interpreter; translator; expounder; explainer; demonstrator; commentator; annotator; speaker; mouthpiece; prolocutor; interlocutor; orator
SPONSOR: deponent; warrant; guarantee; promise; assure; vouch for; pledge; commit; endorse; insure
SPOT: mark; place; discover; dirt; blemish; blot
SPREAD: enlarge; disperse; expand; expanse; feast; diverge
SPRING: early; source; strength; recoil; fly; leap; attack; begin; grow; ascend
SPRINKLE: mix; scatter; wet; rain; baptize
SPUR: incite; hasten; sharp; pointed; impulse
SPURIOUS: false; deceptive; illegitimate; erroneous
SPURT: gush; impulse; haste; exertion
SQUARE: honorable; justice; spar; compensate; pay
SQUASH: destroy; flatten; soft; fix
SQUEEZE: contract; embrace; condense
STAB: knife; kill; injure; pain; pierce
STAGE: platform; dais; forum; arena; position; degree
STAGGER: slow; totter; agitate; astonish; affect
STAID: wise; calm; grave
STAIN: paint; color; spoil; dirty; blemish; disgrace
STALE: old; insipid; deteriorated
STALL: abode; lodge; cease; halt; intermission; lull; rest
STAND: exist; permanent; support; resistance; bravery; resist; resolution; reasoning; defend; indication; obstinate; stop; remain
STANDARD: flag; model; degree; mean; rule; measure; good; perfect
STAR: luminary; actor; noble; badge; ornament; decoration; glory; lead; feature; display
START: begin; arise; impulse; move; go; depart; leap; offer; appear
STATELY: grand; proud; pompous
STATUS: position; situation; repute; terms
STAY: remain; wait; continue; stop; cease; rest; prevent; dwell; live
STEADY: uniform; regular; periodic; stable; persevering; unexcitable; cautious
STEP: support; motive; measure; expedient; pace
STEW: food; cook; heat; difficulty; emotion; excitement; annoyance
STIFF: rigid; severe; ugly; affected; haughty; pompous
STIFLE: kill; silence; conceal
STIMULATE: energize; incite; excite; suggest
STING: pain; tingle; excite; anger

STIR: energy; emotion; move; mix; agitate; excite; jail; prison
STOCK: quantity; materials; property; merchandise; money; store; origin; paternity; kinship
STONE: hard; dense; heavy; kill; attack; punish
STOP: end; cease; close; rest; inaction; hinder; prohibit
STORM: crowd; agitation; convulsion; violence; wind; danger; attack; anger; passion; conquer; seize
STRAIN: race; weaken; fatigue; melody; sound; percolate; clean; exaggerate; overrate; exert; effort; stress
STRANGE: unrelated; wonderful; exceptional; ridiculous
STRATEGY: plan; artifice; deception; tactics
STRAY: wander; deviate; disperse
STRENGTH: animality; tenacity; energy; vigor; greatness
STRESS: emphasis; importance; strain; difficulty
STRETCH: expanse; expand; extend; exaggerate; exert; encroach
STRICT: exact; severe; conscientious; orthodox
STRIKE: hit; beat; impress; disobey; resist
STRINGENT: energetic; authoritative; strict; compulsory
STRIP: take; rob; divest; pare; shed
STRONG: great; powerful; healthy; energetic; tough; tasty; pungent; fetid; resolved; severe
STRUT: walk; parade; boast
STUBBORN: strong; hard; obstinate; resistance
STUFF: substance; contents; matter; texture; material; line; expand; overeat; absurdity; unmeaning; trifle; unsubstantial; close
STUMBLE: fall; flounder; fail; err
STUPID: dull; tiresome; unintelligent; credulous; misjudging
SUBJECT: topic; meaning; servant; enthrall; dominate; liable
SUBMERGE: immerse; plunge; steep; destroy
SUBMISSIVE: tractable; humble; enduring
SUBSTANCE: thing; quantity; matter; texture; essence; wealth
SUDDEN: instantaneous; unexpected; transient
SUFFER: pain; allow; feel; endure
SUGGEST: advise; influence; inform; suppose; remind; describe
SULKY: sullen; dejected; discontented; obstinate
SULLEN: sulky; discourteous; gloomy; obstinate
SUNDRY: many; several; divers; various; myriad
SUNNY: warm; cheerful; luminous
SUPERCILIOUS: proud; insolent; scornful; disrespectful
SUPINE: horizontal; inverted; sluggish; torpid
SUPPRESS: destroy; conceal; silence; restrain
SURREPTITIOUS: untrue; deceptive; furtive
SUSPEND: defer; discontinue; hang
SUSPENSE: cessation; uncertainty; expectation; irresolution
SUSPICION: doubt; fear; supposition; incredulity
SUSTAIN: endure; aid; preserve; support; continue

SWEET: lovely; agreeable; clean; sugary; saccharine; candy
SWELL: increase; expand; extol; fop; noble
SYMPATHY: condolence; pity; kindness; love; friendship; concord
SYNONYM: identity; meaning; interpretation; term

T

TACKLE: undertake; manage; try; gear; fastening
TACT: wisdom; skill; taste; touch; discrimination
TAINT: disgrace; decay; dirty; imperfection
TAKE: eat; believe; know; understand; receive; appropriate; capture; seize; subtract; remove
TAKE DOWN: depress; record; write; dismantle; humiliate; censure
TAKE IN: include; shorten; understand; deceive; receive
TAKE OFF: mimic; ridicule; destroy; remove; divest; depart; discount
TAKE TO: like; love; desire
TAKE UP: elevate; inquire; dissent; choose; undertake; defraud; arrest; borrow; censure
TALK: speak; orate; conversation; rumor
TALK BIG: boast; threaten; insolence
TALK OF: signify; publish; intend
TAME: inert; moderate; domesticate; teach; feeble; subjugate; calm; insensible
TAMPER: alter; seduce; injure; meddle
TANGIBLE: useful; sufficient; exact; material
TARGET: bullseye; mark; destination; point; butt; goal; aim
TARNISH: disgrace; deface; soil; discolor
TAX: inquire; employ; fatigue; compel; request; accuse; import; duty
TEACH: instruct; educate; direct; tutor; guide; prepare; train; lecture; edify; school; coach; enlighten; inform; inculcate; indoctrinate; infuse; instill
TEAR: separate; part; detach; rupture; sever; lacerate; cleave; dissect; slit; divide; cut; rend; slash; rush; rampage; run wild; fly; race; short; whisk; whiz; fame; rage; rave; cry; weep; sob; blubber
TELL: speak; inform; relate; describe; succeed
TEMPEST: storm; wind; agitation; violence; excitement
TEMPT: entice; seduce; allure; fascinate; charm; coax; lure; suggest; attempt; try; essay; endeavor; strive; tackle
TENACITY: toughness; resolution; obstinacy; courage
TENDER: compassionate; affectionate; susceptible; soft; painful; slight; offer; vessel; ship
TENOR: meaning; course; direction; degree; singer
TERM: end; close; conclusion; period; rank; station; stage; seep; degree; duration; space; span; limit; name; call; denominate; designate; dub; specify; settlement

TERMS: conditions; reasoning; circumstances; pacification
(COME TO) TERMS: ascent; pacify; submit; consent; agree
TERRIFY: frighten; astound; appall; horrify
TEST: experiment; attempt; trial; tryout; proof; criterion; diagnose; assay; check; feeler; sample; prove; verify
THEME: subject; topic; thesis; text; point; case; dissertation; essay
THESIS: theme; proposition; dissertation
THICK: crowded; numerous; broad; dense; turbid; dirty
THIN: subduct; few; small; narrow; rare; scant
THIRST: hunger; crave; lust; itch; hanker
THOROUGH: full; absolute; undivided; solid; complete
THROW: impel; propel; exert; reject; eject
THRUST: push; attack; insert; interpose
THWART: obstruct; oppose; cross; harm
TICKLE: amuse; please; touch
TIDY: arrange; orderly; good; clean; pretty
TIE: fasten; secure; hinder; restrain; relation; obligation; cravat
TIME: instant; early; duration; age; now; leisure; inaction; course; destiny
TIME HONORED: old; respected; reputable
TIMID: fearful; cowardly; humble
TINSEL: glitter; sham; ornament; frippery
TIP: end; summit; give; gratuity; reward
TIRADE: oration; recitation; speech; lecture; harangue; disapprobation; diatribe; clamor; outcry
TIRE: weary; fatigue; worry
TITLE: name; indication; distinction; right
TOLERATION: laxity; lenient; permission; feeling; calmness; benevolence
TOMFOOLERY: absurdity; amusement; ostentation; wit
TONE: state; strength; tendency; sound; color; method
TONE DOWN: moderate; darken; discolor
TOOL: instrument; ornament; catspaw; servant
TOWERING: huge; high; large; great; furious
TRACE: mark; record; delineate; inquire; discover; some; smallness
TRADE: traffic; exchange; business
TRAIN: teach; educate; prepare; accustom; vehicle; series; sequence
TRAIT: mark; appearance; specialty; description
TRAMP: stroller; idler; vagabond; bum; hobo
TRANQUIL: calm; quiet; peaceful
TRANSACTION: event; occurrence; incident; affair; proceeding; job; dealings; doings; step; maneuver; compact; contract; agreement; bargain; deal
TRANSGRESS: sin; violate; infringe; go beyond
TRANSLATE: interpret; transfer; resurrect
TRAPPINGS: clothes; equipment; ornaments; adjunct

166

TREACHERY: perfidy; knavery; roquery; rascality; unfairness; villainy; betrayal; dishonesty; fraudulent

TREAT: pleasure; bargain; delight; amuse; manage

TREMBLE: shake; fluctuate; fear

TREPIDATION: fear; excitement; agitation

TRIAL: inquiry; experiment; essay; difficulty; adversity; suffering; lawsuit

TRIBE: race; clan; class; assemblage

TRIBUNAL: court; board; bench; judiciary; forum; bureau; senate; assize

TRICK: artifice; contrivance; deception; roguery; skill; trait; amuse; ridicule; deceive

TRIFLE: small; unimportant; neglect; deceive; disrespect

TRIP: jaunt; run; leap; fall; fail; bungle; mistake; deceive; overthrow

TRITE: hackneyed; commonplace; conventional; familiar; banal; set; regular; stereotyped

TRIUMPH: win; succeed; exult; celebration; boast

TRIVIAL: trifling; useless; unmeaning

TROUBLE: disorder; derange; difficulty; adversity; pain

TRUCE: pacification; peace; cessation

TRUE: real; straight; accurate; veracious; faithful; honorable; orthodox

TRY: experiment; use; endeavor; contend

TUMBLE: fall; derange; agitate; fail

TUMULT: disorder; agitation; revolt

TURBULENCE: violence; agitation; excitement

TURN: crisis; change; deviate; rotate; circuition; tendency; form

TURN AWAY: eject; avoid; dismiss; relinquish

TURN OUT: become; happen; exterior; eject; strike; dismiss; display

TURN OVER: give; invert; entrust; change; improve; repent

TURNING POINT: end; crisis, occasion; reversion; cause; limit

TUSSLE: contention; fracas; discord; shindy; scuffle; broil; fray; scrimmage

TWIST: join; thread; distort; deviate; bend; convolution

TYPE: essential; similiarity; pattern; class; form; indication; letter; print

U

UGLY: homely; ordinary; unsightly; uncomely; unshapely; unlovely; course; garish; misshapen; monstrous; crooked; graceless; inelegant; ungraceful; ungainly; awkward; squalid; grisly; ghastly; gruesome; frightful; hideous; odious; repulsive; horrible; foul; dirty; deformed; disfigured; discolored; blemished

ULTIMATUM: terms; requisition; intention

UMBRELLA: covering; shade; protection
UNABASHED: insolent; vain; bold
UNNACCOUNTABLE: exceptional; irresponsible; arbitrary; unintelligible
UNAFFECTED: genuine; sincere; simple
UNAUTHROIZED: lawless; undue; prohibited
UNBECOMING: incongruous; disreputable; dishonorable; undue
UNBROKEN: entire; continuous; preserved; unviolated
UNCONDITIONAL: complete; free; permission; consent; release
UNDECIDED: uncertain; irresolute; inquiring
UNDER: less; below; covered; hidden
UNDERMINE: burrow; weaken; damage; hinder
UNDERSTANDING: intelligence; agreement; pacification; compact
UNDETERMINED: uncertain; irresolute; chance
UNDO: untie; reverse; destroy; neutralize
UNEARTH: disinter; discover; inquire; eject
UNEQUIVOCAL: great; sure; clear
UNFAIR: unjust; dishonorable; false
UNFIT: inappropriate; wrong; undue; unskilled; impotent
UNFOLD: straighten; evolve; interpret; disclose; manifest
UNFRIENDLY: opposed; hostile; malevolent
UNHEARD OF: exceptional; improbable; wonderful; ignorant
UNIFORM: dress; livery; homogeneous; simple; orderly; regular; symmetry
UNIMPEACHABLE: true; certain; approved; innocent
UNINTERRUPTED: continuous; perpetual; unremitting
UNION: marriage; concord; concurrence; junction; agreement; combination
UNIQUE: dissimilar; original; exceptional; alone
UNITE: join; marry; combine; assemble; concur; converge
UNITY: concord; single; complete; whole; uniformity
UNJUSTIFIABLE: wrong; wicked; inexcusable
UNLIMITED: free; infinite; great
UNMISTABLE: certain; manifest; intelligible
UNMITIGATED: complete; violent; great
UNNECESSARY: redundant; useless; inexpedient
UNNERVED: dejected; weak; powerless
UNOCCUPIED: untenanted; vacant; inactive
UNPARALLELED: exceptional; supreme; unimitated
UNPOLISHED: rough; inelegant; vulgar; rude
UNRAVEL: untie; straighten; evolve; discover; interpret
UNREASONABLE: impossible; illogical; foolish; unjust; exorbitant
UNRUFFLED: calm; quiet; placid; unaffected
UNRULY: violent; obstinate; disobedient
UNSEEN: hidden; invisible; latent
UNSTABLE: changeable; uncertain; irresolute; precarious

UNSULLIED: clean; honorable; guiltless
UNTENABLE: powerless; undefended; illogical
UNWARRANTED: illogical; illegal; undue
UNWIELDY: large; heavy; cumbersome; difficult
UNYIELDING: tough; resolute; obstinate; resisting
UP: vertical; aloft; excited; effervescing
UP TO: brave; skillful; knowing; equal; sufficient; good; due
UP HOLD: continue; support; aid; praise
UPROAR: noise; disorder; violence
UPSET: destroy; invert; defeat; excite; disconcert
URGE: impel; incite; beg; hasten; violence
URGENT: required; important; necessary
USED UP: deteriorated; fatigued; weary; satiated
USUAL: general; ordinary; customary
UTTER: speak; disclose; publish; distribute; extreme

V

VACANT: void; absent; unmeaning
VACATE: displace; absent; depart; resign
VACILLATE: waver; undulate; changeable
VAGARY: absurdity; whim; antic; imagination
VAGUE: unsubstantial; uncertain; unreasoning; unmeaning; obscure
VALID: confirmed; true; sufficient; strong; powerful
VALUE: measure; estimate; importance; utility; goodness; price
VANDAL: brute; rowdy; ruffian; blackguard; hun; goth; destroyer
VARIANCE: difference; disagreement; discord
VARY: change; fluctuate; differ
VAST: great; spacious; large
VEIL: cover; shade; conceal; hide
VENAL: stingy; selfish; dishonest
VENDOR: merchant; seller; salesman; peddler; trader; dealer;
monger; chandler; tradesman
VENERABLE: old; aged; respected; sage
VENOMOUS: bad; poisonous; rude
VERVE: imagination; vigor; energy; feeling
VESTED: legal; fixed; given; due
VICTIMIZE: deceive; baffle; injure; kill
VIEW: sight; appearance; opinion; intention
VIGILANCE: care; wisdom; activity
VIGOR: strength; energy; activity; resolution
VILE: bad; painful; disgraceful; vicious; dishonorable
VILIFY: shame; censure; detract; malediction

VINDICATE: justify; warrant; exonerate; acquit; excuse; pardon; apologize
VIRULENCE: noxiousness; discourtesy; anger; malevolence
VISTA: convergence; sight; appearance; expectation
VIVACIOUS: active; sensitive; cheerful
VOICE: sound; cry; speak; express; promulgate
VOUCHER: indication; security; payment
VOUCHSAFE: permit; censent; condescend; ask
VULGAR: coarse; ribald; unpresentable; uncivil; ill-bred; ill-mannered; ungentlemanly; unladylike; uncouth; rude; gaudy; tawdry; obtrusive; loud; flashy; garish

W

WAGER: bet; chance; risk; venture; hazard; stake; gamble; speculate
WAGES: salary; stipened; allowance; reward; pay; tribute; remuneration; compensation; fee; tip
WALL: vertical; enclosure; obstacle; defense
WANDER: move; journey; deviate
WANE: decrease; contract; decay; age
WANT: desire; poverty; insufficiency; requirement; shortcoming; inferiority
WANTON: unconformable; capricious; unrestrained; rash; impure
WARM: violent; hot; red; ardent; excited; angry; irascible
WARP: change; tend; contract; distort; deviate; deteriorate
WARRANT: promise; security; justify; permit; order; protest; evidence
WARRANTY: sanction; permission; promise; security
WASH: cover; water; cleanse
WASTE: decrease; decrement; destroy; space; plain; spoil; misuse; loss
WATCH: clock; timepiece; observe; see; tend; guard; keep
WATCHMAN: keeper; guardian; sentinel
WAX: increase; become; expand; lubricate
WAY: degree; method; habit; space
(MAKE) WAY: open; avoid; facilitate
WAYWARD: changeable; obstinate; capricious; sullen
WEAK: feeble; insipid; illogical; foolish; irresolate; trifling; lax; compassionate
WEAKEN: decrease; enfeeble; refute
WEAR: clothes; use; decrease; deflect; deteriorate
WEARISOME: laborious, fatiguing; painful
WELL-DEFINED: visible; exact; predetermined
WELL-FOUNDED: existent; probable; certain; true

WHET: sharpen; excite; incite
WHIM: fad; fancy; caprice; desire
WHIP: strike; urge; hasten; flog; scourge
WHITEWASH: acquit; justify; cover; whiten; cleanse
WIELD: use; handle; brandish
WILD: violent; mad; excited; untamed; rash; angry; licentious
WILL: volition; resolution; testament
WINK AT: disregard; neglect; permit; forgive
WINNING: pleasing; courteous; lovable
WISH: will; intention; desire; hope
WISHY WASHY: languid; insipid; feeble; unimportant
WITH: added; mixed; accompanying; means
WITHDRAW: subduct; absent; depart; go; leave; recede; recant; relinquish
WITHHOLD: hide; restrain; prohibit; retain; stint
WRING: twist; torment; pain; clean
WRING FROM: extract; take; compel
WRITHE: pain; agitate; distort
WRONG: error; evil; injury; spite; vice; improper
WRY: pain; discontent; lamentation; ugly

Y

YAMMER: whine; moan; groan
YAP: growl; yarr; yawl; snarl; howl
YARN: filament; story; tale; lie; untruth; exaggeration
YAWN: gape; open; sleepy; tired; weary
YEARN: grieve; repine; pine; droop; languish; mope; brood; desire; wish; fancy; hanker; covet; sympathize
YELL: cry; roar; shout; bawl; hail; whoop; bellow; howl; scream; screech; shriek; squeal; cheer; vociferate; exclaim; thunder; clamor; complain; lament
YIELD: soft; harvest; price; gain; furnish; resign; consent; submit
YOUTH: juvenile; junior; infant; baby; minor; teenager; immaturity; nonage; teens; rising generation; younger generation; young; green; budding; beardless; unfledged; unripe; boy; lad; slip; sprig; stripling; cub; master

Z

ZANY: fool; nincompoop; imbecile; gabby
ZEAL: eagerness; activity; feeling; desire; dogmatism; ardour; earnestness

ZEALOT: dogmatist; bigot; opinionist; enthusiast; fanatic; fan; devotee; hustler; activist

ZENITH: summit; top; vertex; apex; pinnacle; acme; culmination; apogee; greatness

ZIGZAG: oblique; angle; deviate; oscillate

ZONE: region; belt; circle; layer

Words Most Commonly

Mispronounced

by Newsmen

Legend

Ä - as A in arm
Å - as A in ask
Ă - as A in at
Â - as A in air
Ā - as A in ale
Ĕ - as E in ebb
Ē - as E in eel
Ẽ - as E in ermine
Ĭ - as I in it
Ī - as I in ice
Ŏ - as O in odd
Ô - as O in or
Ō - as O in old
OO - as OO in ooze
Û - as U in urge
Ŭ - as U in up
Ū - as U in astūte

174

A

Abdomen: ăb-dō′-měn not ăb′-dō-měn

Abeyance: à-bā′-ăns not à-bē′-ăns

Abhor: ăb-hôr′ not ăb-hor′

Abject: ăb′-jĕkt not ăb-jĕkt′

Absentee: ăb-sĕn-tē′ not ăb′-sĕn-tē

Absorb: ăb-sôrb′ not ăb′-sôrb

Access: ăk′-sĕs not ăk-sĕs′

Acclimate: ăk-klī′-māt not ăk′-klĭm-āt

Accrue: ăk-krōō′ not ăk′-krōō

Across: à-krós′ not à-króst′

Addio: äd-dyō′ not äddēyo′

Adept: äd-ĕpt′ not ăd′-ĕpt

Affix: ăf′-fĭks not ă-fĭks′

Aged (adj.): ā′-jĕd not ājd

Alien: āl′-yĕn not ā′-lĭ-ĕn

Alienate: āl′-yĕn-āt not ā′-lĭ-en-āt

Alloy: ăl-loi′ not ăl′-loi

Allude: ăl-lūd′ not ăl-lōōd′

Ally: ăl-lī′ not ăl′-lī

Amen: ā-mĕn′ not ā′-mĕn

Anew: à-nū′ not à-nōō′

Anti (prefix): ăn′-tĭ not ăn′-tī

Artifice: är′-tĭf-ĭs not är′-tĭf-īs

Ate: āt not ĕt

Azores: à-zōrz′ not ā′-zōrz

B

Bade: băd not bād
Bagnid: băn'-yō not băg'-nĭ-ō
Basket: bȧs'-kĕt not bȧs'-kĭt
Bayou: bī'-ōō not bā'-yū
Blacken: blăk'-n not blăk'-ĕn
Blackguard: blăḡ'-ärd not blăk'-ḡärd
Bombast: bŏm'-bȧst not bŏm-bȧst'
Bona Fide: bō'-nȧ-fī'-dē not bō'-nȧ-fīd
Bristle: brĭs'-l not brĭst'-l

C

Cancel: kăn'-sĕl not kăn'-sl
Canteen: kăn-tēn' not kăn'-tēn
Catch: kăch not kĕch
Celibate: sĕl'-ĭ-bȧt not sĕl-ĭ-bāt'
Chasm: kăzm not kăz'-ŭm
Chasten: chās'-n not chāst'-n
Chastise: chăs-tīz' not chăs'-tīz
Chew: chū not chōō
Chic: shēk not shĭk
Cigar: sĭḡ-är' not sē'-gär
Civil: sĭv'-ĭl not sĭv'-ŭl
Cliche: klē-shā' not klȧ'-shā
Clue: klū not klōō
Cocoa: kō'-kō not kō-kō'-ȧ
Coed: kō-ĕd' not kō'-ĕd
Comely: kŭm'-lĭ not kōm'-lĭ
Comparable: kŭm'-pȧ-rȧ-bl not kŏm-pâr'-ȧ-bl
Contribute: kŏn-trĭb'-ūt not kŏn'-trĭb-ūt
Cosmos: kŏz'-mŏs not kŏz-mōs'
Cousin: kŭz'-n not kŭz'-ĭn
Cupola: kū'-pō-lȧ not kū'-pȧ-lō
Cystitis: sĭs-tī'-tĭs not sĭs-tē'-tŭs

D

Dais: dā'-ĭs not dī'-ĭs
Damage: dăm'-āj not dăm'-ĭj
Data: dā'-tȧ not dä'-tȧ
Datum: dā'-tŭm not dä'-tŭm
Daub: dôb not dŏb
Deaf: dĕf not dēf
Debacle: dā-bäk'-l not dē'-bäk-l
Debauch: dē-bôch' not dē-bowch'
Decade: dĕk'-ād not dĕk-ād'
Decent: dē'-sĕnt not dē'-sŭnt
Decorum: dē-kō'-rŭm not de'-cŏrŭm
Decorative: dĕk'-ō-rā-tĭv not dē-kŏr'-ătĭv
Deduce: dē-dūs' not dē-dōos'
Delirious: dē-lĭr'-ĭ-ŭs not dē-lē'-rĭ-ŭs
Delirium: dē-lĭr'-ĭ-ŭm not dē-lē'-rĭ-ŭm
Delivery: dē-lĭv'-ēr-ĭ not dē-lĭv'-rĭ
Delusion: dē-lū'-zhŭn not dē-lōo'-zhŭn
Demise: dē-mīz' not dē-mēz' or dĕm'-īze
Demolition: dĕm-ō-lĭsh'-ŭn not dē-mō-lĭsh'-ŭn
Deplorable: dē-plō'-rȧ-bl not dē-plŏr'-ȧ-bl
Depths: dĕpths not dĕps
Despicable: dĕs'-pĭk-ȧ-bl not dē-spĭk'-ȧ-bl
Dessert: dĕz-zẽrt' not dē-zẽrt'
Devil: dĕv'-l not dĕv'-ĭl
Devilish: dĕv'-l-ĭsh not dĕv'-lĭsh
Diamond: dī'-ȧ-mŭnd not dīm'-mŭnd
Difference: dĭf'-ẽr-ĕns not dĭf'-rĕns
Different: dĭf'-ẽr-ĕnt not dĭf'-rĕnt
Diorama: dī-ō-rä'-mȧ not dī-ō-rā'-mȧ or dī-ō-răm'-ȧ
Disaster: dĭz-ȧs'-tẽr not dĭs-ȧs'-fẽr
Discern: dĭz-ẽrn' not dĭs-ẽrn'
Discourse: dĭs-kōrz' not dĭs'-kōrs'

Discovery: dĭs-kŭv'-ẽr-ĭ not dĭs-kŭv'-rĭ
Disputant: dĭs'-pū-tănt not dĭs-pū'-tănt
Divert: dĭv-ẽrt' not dī-vẽrt'
Divest: dĭv-ĕst' not dī-vĕst'
Drawer: drô'-ẽr not drôr
Dual: dū'-ăl not doō'-ăl
Duel: dū'-ĕl not doō'-ĕl
Duty: dū'-tĭ not doō'-tĭ or dyū'-tĭ

E

Either: ē'-thẽr or ī'-thẽr both are correct
Elixir: ē-lĭk'-sẽr not ĕl'-ĭk-sẽr
English: ĭng'-glĭsh not ēng'-glĭsh or ĕng'-glĭsh
Episodic: ĕp-ĭ-sŏd'-ĭk not ĕp-ĭ-sō'-dĭk
Epitome: ē-pĭt'-ō-mē not ĕp'-ĭ-tōme
Epoch: ĕp'-ŏk or ē'-pŏk both correct
Equanimity: ē-kwȧ-nĭm'-ĭt-ĭ not ĕk-wȧ-nĭm'-ĭt-ĭ
Equapage: ĕk'-wĭ-pā̇j not ē-kwĭp'-ā̇j
Equitable: ĕk'-wĭ-tȧ-bl not ē-kwĭt'-ȧ-bl
Errata: ĕr-rā'-tȧ not ē-răt'-tȧ
Even: ēv'-n not ēv'-ĕn
Every: ĕv'-ẽr-ĭ or ĕv'-rĭ both correct
Evil: ē'-vl not e'-vĭl
Exit: ĕks'-ĭt not ĕgg'-zĭt
Exploit: ĕks-ploit' not ĕks'-ploit
Extricable: ĕks'-trĭk-ȧ-bl not ĕks-trĭk'-ȧ-bl
Extrude: ĕks-troōd' not ĕks-trūde'

F

Fellow: fĕl'-ō not fĕl'-lẽr
Fertile: fẽr'-tĭl or fẽr'-tīl both correct
Fetish: fē'-tĭsh or fĕt'-ĭsh both correct
Fiasco: fē-ȧs'-kō not fī-ȧs'-kō
Finance: fĭn-ăns' not fī-năns'
Finis: fī'-nĭs not fĭn'-nĭs

Finite: fī'-nīt not fĭn'-ĭt
Flaccid: flăk'-sĭd not flăs'-ĭd
Flew: flū not floo
Flower: flow'-ẽr not flowr
Flue: flū not floo
Flute: flūte not floot
Forbade: fŏr-băd' not fŏr-bād'
Forte (N): fōrt
Forte (adj.): fôr'-tā
Foyer: fwȧ-yā' not foi'-ẽr
Fuel: fŭ'-ĕl not fŭ'-ŭl
Fungi: fŭn'-jī not fŭng'-gī

G

Gala: gā'-lȧ not găl'-ȧ
Ghoul: gool not gowl
Gnome: nōm not ḡ-nōm'-ē
Golden: gōld'-n not gōld'-ĕn
Gosling: gŏz'-lĭng not gŏs'-lĭng
Gossamer: gŏs'-ȧ-mẽr not gŏz'-ȧ-mẽr
Gout: gowt not goot
Grandchild: grănd'-chīld not grăn'-chīld
Granddaughter: grănd'-dô-tẽr not grăn'-dô-tẽr
Grandeur: grăn'-dūr not grăn'-jŭr
Gratis: grā'-tĭs not grăt'-ĭs
Greasy: grēz'-ĭ or grēs'-ĭ both are correct
Gridiron: grĭd'-ī-ŭrn not grĭd'-ī-rŭn
Gristle: grĭs'-l not grĭz'-l
Gyroscope: jī'-rō-skōp not gī'-rō-skōp

H

Habeas Corpus: hā'-be-ăs not hăb'-bē-ăs
Ha-Ha: hă-hä' not hä'-hä
Handbook: hănd'-book not hăn'-book

Handcuff: hănd-kŭf not hăn′-kŭf
Handkerchief: hănd′-kĕr-chĭf not hănk′-ĕr-chĕf
Handsome: hăn′-sŭm not hănd′-sŭm
Harass: hăr′-ăs not hȧ-răs′
Heaven: hĕv′-n not hĕv′-ĕn
Heinous: hā′-nŭs not hē′-nŭs
Herb: ĕrb or hĕrb both are correct
Heretic: hĕr′-ē-tĭk not hĕr′-ĕ-tĭk
History: hĭs′-tō-rĭ not hĭs′-trĭ
Hoist: hoist not hīst
Hoof: ho͞of not hŏͦof
Hospitable: hŏs′-pĭt-ȧ-bl not hŏs-pĭt′-ȧ-bl
Hostage: hŏs-tāj not hōs′-tāj
Human: hū′-măn not yū′-măn
Hussy: hŭz′-ĭ not hŭs′-ĭ
Hustle: hŭs′-l not hŭst′-l
Hygienist: hī′-jĭ-ĕn-ĭst not hī-jĭ-ĕn′-ĭst

I

Ibid: ĭb′-ĭd not ī′-bĭd
Idol: ī′-dŏl not ī′-dl
Illusory: ĭl-lū′-sō-rĭ not ĭl-lū′-zō-rĭ
Image: ĭm′-āj not ĭm′-ĭj
Immediate: ĭm-mē′-dĭ-āt not ĭm-mē′-jāt
Immune: ĭm-mūn′ not ĭm′-ūn
Improvise: ĭm-prō-vīz′ not ĭm′-prō-vīz
Indecent: ĭn-dē′-sĕnt not ĭn-dē′-sŭnt
Indian: ĭn′-dĭ-ăn not ĭnd′-yăn
Inertia: ĭn-ẽr′-shĭ-ȧ not ĭn-ẽr′-shȧ
Introit: ĭn-trō′-ĭt not ĭn′-troit
Inversion: ĭn-vẽr′-shŭn not ĭn′-vẽr′-zhŭn
Iron: ī′-ŭrn not ī′-rŭn
Irony: ī′-rō-nĭ not ī′-ŭr-nĭ
Irrevocable: ĭr-rĕv′-ō-kȧ-bl not ĭr-rē-vō′-kȧ-bl
Ismailia: ēs-mȧ-ēl-yȧ not ĭs′-mayl-yȧ
Israel: ĭz′-rā-ĕl not ĭz′-rē-ĕl

J

Jejune: jē-jūn' not jā'-jūn
Jeopardy: jĕp'-ård-ĭ not jē-ĕp'-ård-ĭ
Jostle: jŏs'-l not jŏst'-l
Joust: jŭst or jōōst not jowst
Jute: jūt not jōōt

K

Kerchief: kẽr'-chĭf not kẽr'-chĕf
Kismet: kĭs'-mĕt not kĭz'-mĕt

L

Label: lā-bĕl not lā'-bl
Lathe: lāth not lăth
Layette: lā-ĕt' not lā-yĕt'
Length: lĕngth not lĕnth
Lenient: lē'-nĭ-ent or lēn'-yĕnt are both correct
Leprosy: lĕp'-rō-sĭ not lĕp'-rĕs-ĭ
Level: lĕv'-ĕl not lĕv'-l
Lever: lĕ'-vẽr or lēv'-ĕr both are correct
Libel: lī'-bĕl not lī'-bl
Libra: lī'-brà not lē'-brà
Lief: lēf not lēv
Lien: lē'-ĕn or lēn both are correct not lē'-yĕn
Livery: lĭv'-ẽr-ĭ not lĭv'-rĭ
Lure: lūr not lōōr
Lurid: lū'-rĭd not lōō'-rĭd

181

M

Madras: mȧ-dras' not mȧ'-dras
Malice: măl'-ĭs not măl'-ŭs
Manchu: măn-choo' not măn'-chū
Mania: mā'-nĭ-a̤ not mān'-ya̤
Market: mär'-kĕt or mär'-kĭt both are correct
Marvel: mär'-vĕl not mär'-vŭl
Matron: mā'-trŭn not māt'-rŭn
Mauve: mōv not mowve
Meaw: mū not mĭ-ow'
Melodic: mē-lŏd'-ĭk not mĕl-ŏd'-ĭk
Memory: mĕm'-ō-rĭ not mĕm'-rĭ
Menial: mē'-nĭ-ăl or mēn'-yăl both are correct
Mezzo: mĕd'-zō not mĕz'-zō
Mien: mēn not mē'-yĕn
Mobile: mō'-bĭl or mō'-bēl not mō'-bīl
Modest: mŏd'-ĕst not mŏd'-ŭst
Modus Operandi: mō'-dŭs ŏp-ē-răn'-dī not mō'-dŭs ŏp-ĕr-ănd'ī
Monocle: mŏn'-ō-kl not mŏn'-ŏk-l
Morsel: môrs'-l not môrs'-ĕl
Mortal: môrt'-l not môr'-tĭl
Museum: mū-zē'-ŭm not mū'-zē-ŭm

N

Negate: nē-gāt' or nē'-gāt both are correct
Nestle: nĕs-l not nĕst'-l
Neutral: nū'-trăl not noo'-trăl
New Orleans: nū ôr'-lē-ănz not nū ôr-lēnz'
Newspaper: nūz'-pā-pẽr not noos'-pā-pẽr
Novel: nŏv'-l not nŏv'-ĕl
Novice: nŏv'-ĭs not nŏv'-ŭs
Noxious: nŏk'-shŭs not nŏk'-shĭ-ŭs
Nude: nūd not nood

Nuisance: nū'-săns not noo͞'-săns
Nuncio: nŭn'-shĭ-ō not nŭn'-sĭ-ō

O

Obesity: ō-bēs'-ĭt-ĭ not ō-bĕs'-ĭt-ĭ
Obtuse: ŏb-tūs' not ŏb-too͞s'
Occult: ŏk-kŭlt' not ŏk'-kŭlt
Ocelot: ō'-sē-lŏt not ŏs'-sĭ-lŏt
Onerous: ŏn'-ĕr-ŭs not ō'-nĕr-ŭs
Opal: ō'-pl not ō'-păl
Opinion: ō-pĭn'-yŭn not ŏpp'-ĭn-yŭn
Oral: ō'-ràl not ŏr'-rŭl
Ore: ōr not ôr
Orgy: ôr'-jĭ not ôr'-jē or ôr'-gē
Orient: ō'-ri-ĕnt not ôr'-ĭ-ĕnt
Original: ō-rĭj'-ĭn-ăl not ôr'-ĭj-ĭn-ăl
Overt: ō'-vĕrt not ō-vĕrt'

P

Pathos: pā'-thŏs not pāth'-ōs
Patio: pä'-tyō not păt'-ē-ō
Patron: pā'-trŭn or păt'-rŭn both are correct
Pedagogic: pĕd-à-gŏj'-ĭk not pĕd-à-gōj'-ĭk
Pencil: pĕn'-sĭl not pĕn'sl
Peony: pē'-ō-nĭ not pē'-yŏn-ĭ
Peril: pĕr'-ĭl not pĕr'-ŭl
Pestle: pĕs'-l not pĕst'-l
Petition: pē-tĭsh'-ŭn not pĕt-ĭsh'-ŭn
Pillow: pĭl'-ō not pĭl-lĕr or pĭl'-ŭ
Plead: plēd not plĕd
Plenary: plē-nà-rĭ or plĕn-à-rĭ both are correct
Plume: plūm not ploo͞m
Pluto: plū'-tō not ploo͞'-tō
Poem: pō'-ĕm not pō'-ŭm or pō'-ĕm or pōm
Porch: pōrch not pôrch

183

Postpone: pōst-pōn' not pōs-pōn'
Preface: prĕf'-ās not prē-fās'
Prefix: (N) prē'-fĭks; (V) prē-fĭks' never prĕ-fĭks'
Primer (book): prĭm'-ẽr not prī'-mẽr
Prism: prĭzm not prĭz'-ŭm
Proboscis: prō-bŏs'-ĭs not prō-bŏs'-ĭs
Procurator: prŏk'-ū-rā-tẽr not prō-kūr'-ă-tẽr
Profile: prō'-fĭl or prō'-fēl or prō'-fĭl all are correct
Prophecy: prŏf'-ē-sĭ not prŏf'-ē-sĭ
Prosaic: prō-zā'-ĭk not prō-sā'-ĭk
Prostate: prŏs'-tāt not prŏs'-trāt
Protestant: prŏt'-ĕs-tănt not prŏd'-ĕs-tănt
Proviso: prō-vĭ'-zō not prō-vē'-zō
Prussic: prŭs'-ĭk not prōō'-sĭk
Psalm: säm (the P and L are not pronounced)
Publicity: pŭb-lĭs'-ĭt-ĭ not pŭb-lĭs'-ĭt-ē
Puerile: pū'-ẽr-ĭl not pūr'-īle
Pumice: pŭm'-ĭs or pū'-mĭs both are correct
Puree: pü-rā' not pū'-rā

Q

Quality: kwŏl'-ĭt-ĭ not kwŏl'-ĭt-ē
Quay: kē not kwā

R

Raisin: rā'-zn not rā'-zôn
Ratio: rā-shĭ-ō or rā'-shō both are correct
Re (law in re): rē not rā
Really: rē-ăl-ĭ not rē'-lĭ or rē'-lē
Recess: rē-sĕs' not rē'-sĕs
Redemption: rē-dĕmp'-shŭn not rē-dĕm'-shŭn
Renew: rē-nū' not rē-nōō'
Reptile: rĕp'-tĭl or rĕp'-tīl both are correct
Resolute: rĕz'-ō-lūt not rĕz'-ō-lōōt

Respite: rĕs'-pĭt not rē-spīt'
Résumé: rā-zü-mā' not rĕ-zü-mā'
Revelry: rĕv'-ĕl-rĭ not rĕv'-ĕl-rē
Revocable: rĕv'-ō-kȧ-bl not rē-vō'-kȧ-bl
Rhapsody: răp'-sō-dĭ not răp'-sō-dē
Ribald: rĭb'-ăld not rī'-bôld
Risque: rēs-kā' not rĭs-kā'
Roil: roil not rīl
Romance: rō-măns' not rō'-măns

S

Sacrament: săk'-rȧ-mĕnt not sā'-krȧ-mĕnt
Salute: sȧ-lūt' not sȧ-lōōt'
Sarcasm: sär'-kăzm not sär'-kăz-ŭm
Satin: săt'-ĭn not săt'-ŭn
Savage: săv'-āj not săv'-ĭj
Savoy: sȧ-voi' not săv'-oi
Sclerotic: sklē-rŏt'-ĭk not sklĕ-rŏt'-ĭk
Semi: sĕm'-ĭ not sĕm'-ī or sĕm'-ē
Senile: sē'-nīl or sē'-nĭl not sĕn'-īl
Sewer (drain): sū'-ĕr not sōō'-ĕr
Sheik: shēk or shāk both are correct
Siren: sī'-rĕn not sī'-rēn
Sleek: slēk not slĭk
Slew: slū not slōō
Solemn: sŏl'-ĕm not sŏl'-ŭm
Sombrero: sŏm-brā'-rō not sŏm-brĕr'-ō
Specie: spē'-shĭ not spē'-shē
Spree: sprā not sprē
Stodgy: stŏj-ĭ not stō-jĭ
Strata: strā'-tȧ not strä'-tȧ
Student: stū'-dĕnt not stōō'-dĕnt
Stupid: stū'-pĭd not stōō'-pĭd
Suicide: sū'-ĭs-īd not sōō'-ĭs-īd
Suppose: sŭp-ōz' not spōz

Sure: shūr not sho͞or
Sword: sōrd not sôrd
Synod: sĭn'-ŭd not sī'-nŭd
Syringe: sĭr'-ĭnj not sĭr-ĭnj'

T

Table D'Hote: tà-bl-dŏt not tă-bl-dē-ōt'
Tactile: tăk'-tĭl not tăk'-tīl
Tamale: tà-mä'-lĕ not tà-mä'-lē
Teat: tēt not tĭt
Tedious: tē'-dĭ-ŭs or tēd'-yŭs not tē'-jŭs
Temperament: tĕm'-pēr-à-mĕnt not tĕm-prà-mĕnt
Temporarily: tĕm'-pō-rā-rĭl-ĭ not tĕm-pō-rā'-rĭl-ē
Terpsichore: tẽrp-sĭk'-ō-rē not tẽrp'-sĭk-ōr
Textile: tĕks'-tĭl not tĕks'-tīl
Thawing: thô'-ĭng not thôr'-ĭng
Theater: thē'-à-tẽr not thē-ā'-tẽr
Thickening: thĭk'-ĕn-ĭng not thĭk-nĭng
Tiny: tī'-nĭ not tē'-nĭ or tī'-nē
Tirade: tĭr-ād' or tī'-rād both are correct
Toffee: tŏf'-ĭ not tŏf'-fē
Tokyo: tō'-kē-ō not tōk'-ē-ō
Tortoise: tôr'-tŭs or tôr'-tĭs both are correct
Toupee: to͞o-pē' not to͞o-pā'
Toward: tō'-ẽrd or tōrd not twōrd
Tractile: trăk'-tĭl not trăk'-tīl
Transmigration: trăns-mĭ-grā'-shŭn not trăns-mī-grā'shŭn
Travel: trăv'-l not trăv'-ĕl or trăv'-ĭl
Tremor: trē'-mŏr or trĕm'-ŏr both are correct
Trepan: trē-păn' not trĕ-păn'
Trestle: trĕs'-l not trĕs'-tĭl or trĕs'-ĕl
Tribunal: trĭ-bū'-năl not trĭb'-ū-năl
Tribune: trĭb'-ūn not trī'-būn or trĭb-ūn'
Triennial: trī-ĕn'-ĭ-ăl not trī-ĕn'-yăl
True: tro͞o not trū
Tryst: trĭst or trīst both are correct

Tube: tūb not to͞ob or tyo͞ob
Tumor: tū′-mẽr not to͞o′-mẽr
Tune: tūn not to͞on
Tunnel: tŭn′-l not tŭn′-ĕl
Tyrannical: tĭ-răn′-ĭk-ăl not tĭr-ăn′-ĭk-ăl

U

Ultimatum: ŭl-tĭm-ā′-tŭm not ŭl-tĭm-ä′-tŭm
Umbrage: ŭm′-brāj not ŭm′-brij
Unguent: ŭng′-gwĕnt not ŭn′-gwĕnt
Unitarian: ū-nĭt-ā′-rĭ-ăn not ū-nĭt-âr′-ĭ-ăn
Urbanity: ûr-băn′-ĭt-ĭ not ûr-bā′-nĭt-ĭ
Urine: ū′-rĭn not ūr′-ĭn
Used: ūzd not ūst
Usually: ū′-zhū-ăl-ĭ not ū′-zhăl-ĭ
Uterine: ū′-tẽr-ĭn or ū′-tẽr-īn both are correct

V

Vagary: vȧ-gā′rĭ not vā′-gȧ-rĭ
Valet: văl′-ĕt or văl′-ā both are correct
Vapid: văp′-ĭd not vā′-pĭd
Varicose: văr′-ĭ-kōs not văr′-ĭ-kōz
Variety: vȧ-rī′-ē-tĭ not vȧ-rī′-ĕ-tē
Velvet: vĕl′-vĕt or vĕl′-vĭt both are correct
Venerable: vĕn′-ẽr-ȧ-bl not vĕn′-rȧ-bl
Vermouth: vẽr′-mo͞oth not vẽr-mo͞oth′
Version: vẽr′-shŭn not vẽr′-zhŭn
Vertebra: vẽr′-tē-brȧ not vẽr′-tȧ-brȧ
Vessel: vĕs′-ĕl not vĕs′-l or vĕs′-ĭl
Via: vī′-ȧ or vē′-ȧ both are correct
Victim: vĭk′-tĭm not vĭk′-tŭm
Victual: vĭt′l not vĭk′-tū-ăl
Violent: vī′-ō-lĕnt not vī′-ō-lĭnt
Virile: vĭr′-ĭl or vī′-rĭl never vĭr-īl′

Viscount: vī'-kownt not vĭs'-kownt
Visor: vĭz'-ẽr or vī'-zẽr both are correct
Volatile: vŏl'-à-tĭl never vŏl'-à-tīl
Volume: vŏl'-ūm not vŏl'-yŭm
Voyage: voi'-āj not voi'-ĭj

W

Wandering: wŏn'-dẽr-ĭng not wŏn'-drĭng
Wary: wā'-rĭ or wâr'-ĭ both are correct
Was: wŏz not wŭz nor wôz
Water: wô'-tẽr not wŏt'-ẽr
Wednesday: wĕnz'-dā not wĕn'-ĕs-dā
Whack: hwăk not wăk
Whale: hwāl not wāl
What: hwŏt not wŏt
When: hwĕn not wĕn
Why: hwī not wī
Widow: wĭd-ō not wĭd-ŭ
Wizen: wĭz'-n not wīz'-ĕn
Women: wĭm'-ĕn or wĭm-ĭn both are correct
Wrestle: rĕs'-l not rĕst'-l nor răs'-l

Y

Yellow: yĕl-ō not yĕl-ŭ
Yesterday: yĕs'-tẽr-dā not yĕs-tẽr'-dā

Z

Zany: zā'-nĭ not zā'-nē
Zoological: zō-ō-lŏj'-ĭk-ăl not zōō-ō-lŏj'-ĭk-ăl
Zoologist: zō-ŏl'-ō-jĭst not zōō-ŏl'-ō-jĭst
Zouave: zōō-äv' or zwäv both are correct

188

Index